HAMPSTEAD

Fragments

Of

Remembrance

Finding Lost Boys

Edited by

Jonathan Nicholls

With a Foreword by

John Grieve CBE QPM

First edition published in 2022 by Hampstead Pals Productions
Copyright 2022 Jonathan Nicholls

All rights reserved
ISBNs:
978-1-80227-514-8 (Paperback)
978-1-80227-513-1 (Hardback)
978-1-80227-515-5 (eBook)

Typeset and produced by PublishingPush.com

Contents

John Street	-	Michael Jackson
Alexander Nigel Trotter	-	Jonathan Nicholls
Jack Turner	-	Trevor Bettles
George Ward	-	Judith Rushby
Arthur Whitrod	-	Eugenie Brooks
Roper Whitrod	-	Eugenie Brooks
John Patrick Hickie	-	John Hickie MBE

3. The Great Silence – The Veterans
John Joseph Cousins MM
Bill Hay
Bill Partridge
Alf Razzell
Charles Taylor

4. These names will be found again -   Jon Buoy
Harry Alexander
Dave Gallaher
Danny Lambert
Edgar Mobbs
Tommy Nelson
James Pearson
Jack Raphael
Frank Tarr
Alexander Todd
Phillip Waller

5. The Hares of the Somme

Acknowledgements

Further acknowledgements.

With Eternal Gratitude to
THE COMMONWEALTH WAR GRAVES COMMISSION
For Keeping Watch

By Jonathan Nicholls

'CHEERFUL SACRIFICE'
The Battle of Arras 1917
Available on Amazon

'THAT BLOODY BAND'
Available on Amazon

Foreword
Professor John Grieve CBE QPM

Deputy Assistant Commissioner Metropolitan Police (Rtd)

This is a story of the many pilgrimages by one group of Pals to find lost boys. Whilst three family stories and one Police colleague's story recorded here are of Victoria Cross winners, the majority are of ordinary men torn from their families who died in the hellish conditions that were the so-called 'Great War', later called 'World War I' and, even later, the 'Great European Civil Wars 1914-1946'.

The majority of the family and Pals narratives here are about 1914 - 1918 but three are about 1939 - 1945; one of these is about another Victoria Cross winner from that war. Without being pretentious, this is a book about truly modern-day pilgrimages; it is our contemporary version, which is probably more inspired by Chaucer and to Canterbury than to Carmina Santiago de Compostela. It is about remembrance; it is about families, love, life and loss, comradeship, friendship, courage, sacrifice, poetry, memory, history, music, drink, food, and much, much else.

Jon Nicholls has written below of the very early days of the Hampstead Pals, and it is the contribution of Jon himself in creating these modern pilgrimages and his strategic and tactical commentary on each entry.

"We realised then, that our troubles were little ones. It became clear. Life was meant for *living to the full* and enjoying it to the limit. There seemed no point in worrying over the minor irritations and dramas of modern life. It changed our outlook. Those lads in the cemeteries never had the chance of the good life we enjoy today but they gave the greatest thing a man can give - *Life itself*. And they gave it for us... and that is the driving force of remembrance which lies behind the Hampstead Pals. From 1979 until 1993, we always took veteran soldiers of that terrible conflict with us. The story of their return to their battlefields is recorded in this book."

His statement above mirrored my own experience with the Hampstead Pals. Although I had met Jon long years before, through the agency of Dick West when we were all Sergeants Three (sic), I did not go on a Pals trip until the late 1990s. When I did go, eventually reintroduced by Dick to Flanders and Picardy with the Pals, I was the Metropolitan Commissioner of Police's crisis-buster and forever attempting (metaphorically) to put out fires. My recognition, like Jon's, in that first cemetery I visited (shown here on this book's front cover), was that our fires, individually and often, as police officers, were as nothing compared to this greatest of all conflagrations. As my friend and colleague former CIA chief Dick Kerr puts it in his introduction here, "I was in for an emotional shock". One shock after another hit me. I returned to my Police tasks, among which was rejigging our response to bereaved families and devastated communities, with renewed empathy.

I do not agree that this book of family pilgrimages is 'parochial', as one reviewer wrote, and I have been thinking about the global significance of what the 25 plus (out of more than 350 Hampstead Pals pilgrims in nearly 50 years) have written here. 'Parochial' might also imply too local and chatty, yet Jon deals with that in his strategic editorial notes. The contributors are writing of the role of the 'little people' in the affairs of the so-called 'mighty' (to misquote J.R.R. Tolkien in the *Lord of the Rings*) 'and we have travelled in his footsteps and those of his lost boys on the dead marshes of the Somme'.

On that first trip, Jon introduced me to many books, the copies of which are before me on my shelves, but, foremost of all, 'Before Endeavours Fade' written by Rose Coombes MBE. She was Special Collections Officer at the Imperial War Museum and "undoubtedly, the greatest guide" and hugely knowledgeable of the Western Front of 1914-18. I have a recording of her interviewing my dad about his experiences in World

War 2. Her ashes were scattered at Ypres and there is a road up to the cemetery named after her. I had read the 'Big Three's' books (those of Sassoon, Graves and Blunden) but here was something different; an encyclopaedic labour of immense love and vast remembrance, epitomised by the initials of her title, 'BEF', which also stands for British Expeditionary Force.

This book is another labour of love. Again, I can do no better than quote Jon:

> "It is the simple but moving, personal stories that form the backbone of this book. They concern lost and still much-loved family members. A grandfather, an uncle, a great-uncle... They are about ordinary families fractured by war. This loss still resounds down the generations, over one hundred years later. Their stories are preserved here - for posterity and for their families. We must never forget."

We have been so fortunate to do so much with the Pals over the last 25 years. I have attended Diva classes on Poets and Pals, I have stood with Tony Spagnoly and heard the finer minute tactical details of trench raids and their medieval ferocity and heard him read his poems. I have walked battlefields and visited cemeteries, graves of men and women, right down the vast sweep of the Old Front Line from Calais to Verdun. I have trod the beaches of Dieppe, Normandy and Gallipoli, I have visited Troy with Pals and seen Homer's 'wine-dark sea' (and drunk lots of it with them). With Pals, I stood where Caesar stood, where the Black Prince earned his spurs, where Henry V defied the Constable of France, where Wellington, Marlborough, and Napoleon rode, and where Frost defied the armoured columns of the Nazi SS at Arnhem. But the core, the absolute core of what the Pals do is to stand in those cemeteries, large and small, amongst those lost boys and girls of 1914 - 1918 to hear the larks sing again and to remember them.

So, for me, finally, herein are the thoughts of being with Caroline Carr and her mother, Jacqui Downing, when, on visiting their Uncle Charlie's grave with us, we came across that of a lost stranger, a Private Thomas Palmer of the 1/4 Leicesters, killed in February 1917. What happened next said it all. One of his parents had chosen this moving inscription on his grave:

'Will some kind hand in a foreign land place a flower on my son's grave'.

I watched that day as the kind hands of those two Hampstead Pals, those pilgrims, gathered nearby wild flowers and did just that. That epitomises for me what this book is all about.

It is a bundle of flowers placed on a lost child's grave.

Introduction
Paul Nicolas.

Former Police Commander & Regional Director of General Intelligence
Lorraine & Metz
FRANCE

When my friend, Jon Nicholls, asked me in early 2021 to contribute to his new writing project, a book about remembrance of fallen soldiers of the Great War and The Hampstead Pals, I immediately agreed. How can I refuse, after a friendship that has bound us for over thirty years?

Our first meeting dates back to the early 1980s when I joined the Pals in Albert with my colleague José Heussner, to visit sites of the Great War 1914-18, built to the glory of the British Army and its allies in this region of Picardy, which was deeply scarred during the Somme Battle of 1916. The trip was under the International Police Association, and, together with his group of Hampstead Police Officers, we travelled through several battlefields and places of remembrance. The memorials at Longueval, Beaumont-Hamel and Thiepval bear witness with strength and pride to the courage but also to the sacrifice of all those soldiers who came to my country to defend our freedoms.

The following years were a real pleasure, as I regularly joined the Hampstead Pals to explore other areas of Northern France marked by the 1914-1918 conflict. Péronne, Arras, Lorraine, Verdun and the Forts of Vaux, Douaumont and Souville are all symbolic places, as well as Ypres and Mons in Belgium.

From these visits, I remember the veteran soldiers, such as Alf Razzell, who gave us colourful details about his life as a soldier. These sacred places and the solemnity of the ceremonies of remembrance at some graves perpetuate forever our Franco-British friendship which is represented by the commemorative poppy flower. Emotional moments that I will remember for evermore.

The atmosphere was just superb when the Hampstead Pals came to Lorraine to visit the battlefields of Verdun and its surroundings. In 1990, the Hampstead Pals crossed the border into Germany and we visited German colleagues in Saarbrücken and then to Metz and our Police HQ which further consolidated the strong bonds of friendship between our two countries.

Let us hope that better days will come to allow a beautiful reunion in order to perpetuate these acts of remembrance and our deep Franco-British friendship.

Preface
Richard J. 'Dick' Kerr

Former Deputy Director of the Central Intelligence Agency (CIA)
USA

A cut at my thoughts about the Hampstead Pals trip.

As the American member of the four-man Independent Monitoring Commission, I had learned how important it was to follow the lead of John Grieve. So, when he suggested that I join the Hampstead Pals on their trip to the WWI battlefields, the answer was clearly an enthusiastic 'yes'!

I had a smattering of knowledge about WWI and the trench warfare along the Somme, but, as was the case with most Americans, details were missing and I had no emotional connection with those who perished. What would remain from a war fought nearly a hundred years ago? I saw open fields, a few monuments here and there, some cemeteries and little else. I was in for an emotional shock.

The story of the conflict was told by visiting the graves of the young men who died in the conflict but who left their poems, letters and individual stories in the hands of the next generations - among them, The Hampstead Pals - keeping their memories alive. Their stories were read aloud at the head of graves at the site of their death.

It was not just mourning but a call out to remember their lives

Hampstead Pals & The Great War.

Jon Nicholls writes;

The smell of strong coffee combined with pungent Gauloises cigarette smoke takes me back to that lively little bar of the 'Relais Fleuri' in Albert, France. It is, of course, a rare thing to catch a whiff of that intriguing aroma nowadays. Smoking is now banned from all French bars (although not all French establishments comply with EU regulations) and the youth of France has been cultured in the health hazards of Turkish tobacco, which old soldier Alf Razzell amusingly referred to as 'smoking camel shit.'

It was around 1981 that Alf - once a Royal Fusilier - first sailed to France with the enigma known as the 'Hampstead Pals.' So, who are the Hampstead Pals?

A leading article by Sue Corbett in *The Times* Newspaper of Saturday 3 November 2012 best gives a clue;

> "Over beans on toast in the Hampstead Police Station canteen one September morning 35 years ago, a 29-year-old police sergeant, Jon Nicholls, was holding forth enthusiastically about the five days he had just spent exploring the First World War battlefields and cemeteries of the Somme. Somewhat to his surprise, he found that he had tapped into the remarkable affinity that many serving and retired police officers seem to feel with the men and boys who, nearly 100 years ago, served with the British Expeditionary Force.
> The upshot was that Nicholls and ten colleagues decided to form a travel club of police officers and their friends, dedicated to making regular pilgrimages to significant First World War sites in France and Belgium. At the suggestion of a Great War veteran whom Nicholls met by chance while on patrol, they called the club *The Hampstead Pals* in memory of the Pals' Battalions in which friends, neighbours and workmates served together in the war...

So, that was it. It could not be more eloquently summed up and I well remember that breakfast meeting clearly. I was early-turn 'Station Officer' at Hampstead Police Station when I was joined at the canteen breakfast table by my fellow sergeant, Peter Dumville.

I had held a lifelong interest in - or rather an obsession with - the Great War of 1914-18 and I told Peter that I had just returned from a short but evocative 'pilgrimage' with my wife to the battlefields of the Somme in Northern France. It was my first visit to that beautiful yet mysterious land called France. I had 'blindly' driven there, precariously and terrifyingly on the wrong side of the road, in a clapped-out Vauxhall Viva, staying four nights at a little roadside lorry drivers hotel in Albert, which we found more by luck in the throes of a wedding party on a hot summer's afternoon, which was congaing out onto the Bapaume road.

'That's something I have always wanted to do, Nick,'- as Peter always called me - 'I have always wanted to visit the battlefields and cemeteries of the First World War.' Peter Dumville was a dependable and useful friend. Not only was he an experienced 'skipper' but he was the secretary of *Hampstead Police Social Club,* and, as it happened, I had just been elected onto the social club 'committee'.

It was decided, there and then, that it would be a great idea to form a small battlefield 'remembrance' group. We would soon call ourselves 'The Hampstead Pals' at the suggestion of old soldier Bill Hay. We promptly suggested that the rich Hampstead Police Social Club should provide some funding. This proposition or 'motion' was unanimously carried at the next meeting of 'EH' social club one week later, when the committee decided that the social club would pay for the £300 hire of the mini-bus from St Alban's Van Hire, to carry us eager pilgrims of the Great War to France. All five members of the committee came. This generous committee would later finance the return of several Great War veterans to their old action spots of 1914-18.

Eleven Metropolitan police officers from Hampstead Division subsequently set off for France, in May 1979, to the 1916 Battlefields of the Somme.

Only two of us had ever been to France before. All of us had fathers and grandfathers who had fought in that battle. Most of us had read the evocative 'First Day On The Somme' by Martin Middlebrook. It was a brilliant book that had been my real inspiration to go the previous summer. We were also armed with a battered copy of 'Before Endeavours Fade' by Rose Coombes MBE (The Special Collections officer at the Imperial War Museum and, undoubtedly, the greatest guide and source of knowledge of the Old Western Front of 1914-18). It was the only 'comprehensive' guide to the Western Front at the time and remains, today, still the best. It had been well-thumbed and studied intensely during quiet times when on night duty. Little did we know we would soon meet 'Aunt Rose' Coombes one misty morning in Messines.

Fortunately, she was a rare specimen of humanity who actually *liked* policemen and always, gruffly but fondly, referred to us as, 'My boys'.

That first inspirational trip to the Somme Battlefields was a great adventure in a foreign field. We polished up our schoolboy French and just blindly went. There were no British people living on the Somme offering cheap accommodation. Their time had not yet come. Very few people visited the Somme back then. So, I booked us in where I had stayed the previous summer, at 'Le Relais Fleuri' in Albert. This grubby but friendly little estaminet was owned by Madam Vandeporte, a kindly host. There were no 'en-suite' facilities, just a small bathroom that served us all and we slept four to a room. Some of us never made it to the bedroom and simply slept on the floor of the bar. The food was wonderfully cooked and substantial. The cockerel's head was found in the Coq au vin by Maurice Link. The cheap but delicious vin du pays was delivered daily in one-litre glass bottles and simply plonked on our dining table. It was soon guzzled and properly degreased the chips which were swallowed by the handful. We loved that little estaminet and once our French hosts no longer eyed us with a gallic suspicion, we were treated with incredible kindness. (This had nothing to do with gifts of duty-free cigarettes, whisky and a police helmet.) Le Relais Fleuri would become our regular 'billet' for the next five years.

The days were subsequently spent wandering and exploring the green fields of Picardy and the battlefields and sad British cemeteries of the Battle of the Somme. It had been a sublimely moving experience. It made us spiritually stronger and gave a new meaning to the word 'comradeship', which, in the words of Frederick Manning in his wonderful novel of the Great War, *Her Privates We,* 'rises on occasions to an intensity of feeling which friendship never touches.' Any person with the remotest interest in the First World War should read that book, later renamed - after the profanities were thankfully restored - to 'The Middle Parts of Fortune'.

We hoped that first journey made us better police officers. When we first saw the little cemeteries of the Somme, especially around Railway Hollow near Serre, there was hardly a dry eye amongst us. It is a hard heart that is not moved by the sadness and sheer beauty of these little British graveyards, so caringly maintained by that fine institution, *The Commonwealth War Graves Commission.* We realised then that our troubles were little ones. It became clear. Life was meant for living to the full and enjoying to the limit. There seemed little point in worrying over the minor irritations and dramas of modern life. It changed our outlook. Those lads in the cemeteries never had the chance of the good life we enjoy today but they gave the greatest thing a man can give: *Life itself.* And they gave it for us.

> To face such torments, I would answer; *'You!'*
> Not for themselves, O daughter, grandsons, sons,
> Your tortured forebears wrought this miracle;
> Not for themselves, *accomplished utterly*
> This loathliest task of murderous servitude;
> But just because they realized that thus,
> *And only thus*, by sacrifice, might they
> Secure a world worth living in – For you.

Those inspiring words say everything. Written by Gilbert Frankau, a British officer who served on the Western Front at all the major battles, this stunning extract from one of his poems was taken from his book 'The Other Side and other Poems' (1918). That scrap of verse has never ceased to move me and is the driving force of the ongoing act of remembrance which is The Hampstead Pals.

Every year since that embryo was planted in 1978, The Hampstead Pals have been back to the Western Front and visited all of the old action spots - from Mons to the Armistice, from Arras to Ypres, from Verdun to Gallipoli - (officially) over 75 tours. From 1979 until 1993, we always took veteran soldiers of that terrible conflict with us. The story of their return to their battlefields is recorded in this book.

Today, *The Hampstead Pals* exist as a group of friends dedicated to the remembrance of the sacrifice made by British & Commonwealth Forces in two world wars. Over 350 'Pals' have travelled on our memorable tours and the proud Metropolitan Police connection is still as strong as the day we first went. Many 'Met' Police helmets (a sought-after souvenir) still stand on dusty shelves in French and Belgian bars. The 'Grande Alliance' still survives despite the recent political claptrap from both sides of the channel.

Our pilgrims to the battlefields with The Hampstead Pals have recently included Commissioners, Sir John Stevens and Dame Cressida Dick. Tours are non-profit-making and happen twice a year, although there are occasional smaller pilgrimages by mini-coach. The demand is very high and the tours are always fully booked. There's a constant stream of 'military and police humour' too. As veteran soldier and Somme veteran, Jack Cousins MM, commented, "The laughter still rings in my ears".

This book is neither a battlefield guide nor a war history. There are plenty of those in publication. It simply does what the cover says; 'Fragments of Remembrance' and 'Finding Lost Boys'. It was not written by professional historians or authors. Just ordinary people who came searching for their loved ones. There is no index as it is easy to navigate. There are some fascinating yet very sad stories. Some – mainly the Rugby Union players – have been told before.

We elected to keep all photos in black & white to add to the general 'atmosphere' of the book which is illustrated with the unique and colourful artwork drawn in situ on the battlefields by artist, historian, and top detective, Professor John Grieve CBE QPM.

It is dedicated to our magnificent Commonwealth War Graves Commission.

First Billet Albert 1979

Final Billet Arras 2019

A Hampstead (Police) Pals Production

The popular form of currency used in the early days for getting the Hampstead Pals to the top of the Ulster Tower and to the forbidden corridors of Fort Vaux, Verdun

CHAPTER 1

Wait for me, Grandfather.

The Great Mourning

Brings shadows of distant tree stumps to my bedroom wall,
my twilight world caught between the dark and the light,
scars of shell holes masked under a poppy-grass mascara.

The great furnace lit, I shiver under England's cold sun,
the genetic fragility of fathers, cuts trail in well-worn streets
and firm men walk and toil in their seldom-recognised lives.

A last post lands on my mat, poppy sellers at stations collect;
train late again, smokers cough, steel wheels slide on wet leaf tracks
poppies drip blood into a complex world of manipulated hopes.

My mind wanders, stretching the tethers of the minute's silence.
Over Cenotaph's blood-soaked roots, sombre politicians slide
on the wet lines of their pedigree fathers, they so solemnly bow.

Wait for me, grandfather, where pigeons meander between lamp posts
forever pecking morsels from long lines of deep pavement cracks:
stump legs, milky eyes, broken wings, flightless dreams.

On the station forecourt, a smell of cigarette smoke undoes my resolve,
a confidently lit third light. Gone now those bleak thoughts of dying days,
no bullets to fear here as in your earlier time of such precious moment.

My train held at a red signal, I delve into the deep waters of your life
as I think of you, my grandfather, in your flesh-drenched muddy hole
cherishing every second of luck. I will remember always your bitter recounts.

You read the vinegary wet lines of newspaper wraps on your fish and chips,
resenting the success of the slippery excuses not to stand and fight,
steam from your mouth, like cigarette smoke, from chips too hot to swallow.

All give me insight beneath the smoke of mystical, poppy glaze reflection over
long wet lines of leaden deceit, less palatable than truth for destitute heroes.
To see a white bedroom wall, but not forget the dark stumps of shadows past.

Police Constable Tim Savage, Metropolitan Police.

Sapper Alfred HARRIS

1st /1st (South Midland) Field Company. Royal Engineers
Died of wounds 14 November 1916
Dernancourt Communal Cemetery Extension

Found & commemorated at Dernancourt Communal Cemetery Extension by
grandson Jon Buoy, Senior Master, Mill Hill Prep School (Rtd), who writes;

My grandfather, Alfred Harris, was born in Bristol in 1872. He was the 4th of 12
children and was a cabinet maker by trade. His wife was Elizabeth Amy and the
children were: Sidney, Mabel, Minnie, Arthur and Winifred (my mother).

As a family, we first found Alfred's grave in 1984 whilst holidaying in France with my
wife Janice and our children, Nick and Charlotte. My mother had never visited the
grave until we took her for the first time in 1992 when she was 72 years old. (See inset

photo) She had only met her father, Alfred, the once as a babe in arms during his leave from the front, so you can imagine how emotional this meeting was at the graveside with Mum hugging the gravestone and sobbing. A French farmer in the field opposite sensed the tense moment and stood up in the seat of his tractor and shouted, 'Vive les Anglais!'

It was only when Mum passed away at the tender age of 97 years in 2012 that we found some original letters amongst her things; letters that she had kept and not disclosed to the family in all those years.

The first letter was from Alfred to his wife Elizabeth dated 11 November 1916:

> *Dear Wife,*
>
> *I hope that you are quite well as it leaves me at present; sorry that I could not write before. You know that we have had a great deal to do out here but we make the most of it. I am sending you a silk card. I should like to know if you received the letter from Charlie. But I must tell you I received the papers sent and a letter from you about Sid receiving my postcard. I hope that he is alright.*
>
> *You may rest your mind contented to know that I am thinking of you and that our wedding (anniversary) day is drawing closer and that I am just the same as when we first met. I know that it is a source of trouble to you to think that I am away from you but probably there may come a time someday when we can come together once more. It is a long time to look forward to but you must look on the bright side.*
>
> *Charlie is alright up to the present. I have seen Sam Barrett; he is out where I am. I hope that your leg will be better as soon as possible. You know I always like to hear from you. I was amused at you sending those comic papers, also the Union Jack. I have not much time to read just now but I glanced over the News of the World. I sent on a rosary. I don't know whether you received it or not, so write and let me know if you have. If you are short, I will try and send you something, if possible, later. I must now conclude with fond love and best wishes from all.*
>
> *I must remain your husband Alf.   Xxxxxx*

The second letter is from J Taggart, a medical orderly, informing Elizabeth that Alfred had died in a field hospital in France on 14th November 1916, having been hit by a mortar shell 2 days previously:

South Midland Casualty Clearing Station
B.E.F.
14.11.16
Dear Mrs Harris,
I am very sorry to have to tell you that your husband passed away in this hospital at 5.45 this morning. He was brought in on the 12th severely wounded internally and in spite of every care, he gradually got worse. He talked of you and said how much he would like to see you. He slipped away and suffered no pain. He is buried near the Hospital and if you write to the War Office, a photograph of his grave will be sent to you. His belongings will be sent on as soon as possible. With much sympathy.
Yours sincerely,
J. Taggart.

The third letter was from Major H Clissold, Alfred's Commanding Officer, informing Elizabeth of the details of his death. He had been hit in a dugout in the village of Martinpuich on the 12th November 1916, the day after he had written his last letter to his wife and been badly wounded. He was immediately taken to hospital and died 2 days later.

1st/1st Royal Engineers France, 11/1916
My dear Mrs Harris,
With very deep regret I have to announce to you the sad news of the death of your husband no11 Sapper A Harris.
He was severely wounded while standing in the doorway of his dugout in the village of Martinpuich on the 12th of this month and though he was immediately taken to hospital, I fear there was small chance from the first and he only lived for 3 days. He was an old and tried member of the company who did his duty on all occasions and, in the midst of your grief, you may be proud that he died as a soldier should, at the post of danger, serving his King and Country. His belongings will be sent to you in due course but you must not be surprised if there is some delay.
Your husband will be greatly missed in the Company and on behalf of the Company as well as myself, I want to express to you our deepest sympathy in your sorrow.

Yours sincerely

H Crissold

Major/Adjutant 1st/1st South Midlands RE Company.

Alfred had volunteered very early in the war in 1914 at the age of 44 years, which is shown by his regimental number which was no 11. The regiment was part of the British Expeditionary Force. We have traced his journey across France with the Royal Engineers through the war diaries for his regiment building bridges, making bombs, digging trenches and setting up various installations for his fellow soldiers. This journey ended for him in the village of Martinpuich on the Somme in 1916 when, as part of a working party of four moving up the line, they were hit by a shell.

2nd Lieutenant Clarke, Sergeant Dunk and Lance Corporal Reece were killed instantly and Alfred was badly injured. Very unusually, they were all mentioned by his Commanding Officer by name in the war diary. Usually, only officers were mentioned by name in the war diaries. Alfred's younger brother Charlie, who he made reference to in his letter, survived the war and lived well into his seventies.

We have visited Grandad Harris several times with the Hampstead Pals and shared the story each time alongside his grave at Dernancourt Communal Cemetery, which was close to a hospital clearing station – probably where Alfred was taken after being wounded and where he later died.

More recently, my daughter, having first visited the cemetery in 1984, visited with her family in 2020 to introduce Grandad to three of his great-great-granddaughters. Long may the remembrance continue through the generations.

Sapper Alfred Harris was not a high-ranking, highly decorated soldier but merely a family man doing his duty for King and Country to ensure that we, as later generations, could enjoy the freedom that we often take for granted. He was certainly a hero in our family and will always be remembered.

Editor's note:

The German-held village of Martinpuich, which is to the northeast of High Wood and where Alfred received his fatal wound, was captured by the 15th (Scottish) Division on 15th September 1916, one of the great British Army offensive days of the Battle of the Somme. It is chiefly remembered as a day in which tanks were first used in action, four tanks being employed successfully at Martinpuich. Following the capture of the village, a Decauville light railway line was hastily laid from Martinpuich to Peake Wood, near La Boiselle and it is highly possible that on 11 November, the badly wounded Alfred Harris was taken from Martinpuich to Dernancourt via this light railway system. The village contained the 45th and 56th (1st/1[st]South Midland) Casualty Clearing Stations from September 1916 and the majority of soldiers that died here were laid to rest in the nearby cemetery.

Dernancourt Communal Cemetery Extension.

This attractive two-tiered Somme cemetery is a delight to the eye and was beautifully designed by Sir Edwin Lutyens. It was finally completed in 1925 with the addition of many graves brought in from smaller nearby cemeteries and it now contains 2,162 Commonwealth burials, of which 177 are unidentified. The Hampstead Pals have been here many times and it is sad to think of and see the number of badly wounded men who died here before they could be evacuated by the nearby railway to a main hospital. One of whom was Alf Harris.

In the back row of the cemetery lies Alf Harris's namesake, although no relation, Sergeant TJ Harris VC MM, 6th Royal West Kents, who was killed in action, winning the VC while attacking a German machine-gun post at the nearby village of Morlancourt during the second day of the great Allied offensive of August 1918.

Alf Harris's three comrades of 1/1 Field Company Royal Engineers, killed instantly on 12 November 1916 by that fatal shell, were all Bristol men and are buried together at **Martinpuich British Cemetery.**

Note

The headstone gives Alfred's age as 48 years which is incorrect, as he was, in fact, 42 years old. On it is written; 'God's Will be done'

Corporal Fred HINE
1st Aircraft Depot Royal Air Force
Died of Influenza 9 February 1919
Longuenesse Souvenir Cemetery, St Omer

Found & commemorated at Longuenesse Souvenir Cemetery (St Omer) by grandson
John Hine, Detective Sergeant, Metropolitan Police Flying Squad (Rtd), who writes;

I know very little about my grandfather as his records were destroyed in the London
Blitz. What we do know has been passed down through the family. I regret not talking
to my grandmother about him and the only paperwork we have was rescued from the
bonfire that his father was planning. We walked in just at the right time!

Fred Hine was born in 1877 at 40 College Lane, Stratford upon Avon to Thomas Hine (Labourer) and Sarah Ann Hine, formerly Smith. At some time, Fred moved to Cardiff and lived at 7 Wyndham Road, Canton, Cardiff, after he married my grandmother Harriet in May 1904. They had three children, two of whom survived childhood; Archibald, (Archie, my father) and Edna.

He was a painter and decorator by trade and also quite a talented artist. He played rugby football for Cardiff and was capped three times. The caps represent three seasons when he had to play a certain number of games. In total, he represented Cardiff 44 times.

When I was a serving police officer, I was approached by a colleague, Trevor Blake, to enquire if my grandfather had played rugby for Cardiff and it transpires that our grandfathers not only played together but there is a photo of the team of 1899-1900 with them standing side by side. (Small world!)

Fred originally joined the army in October 1916, when the nation was crying out for men during the Battle of the Somme and he joined the Coldstream Guards at the age of 38 years. It was rumoured that he had been given a white feather in the street.

He transferred to the Royal Air Force and was posted to RAF St Omer in April 1918. At the end of the war, he was kept back in France to help in the 'clearing up' operations and it was at St Omer that he caught Spanish 'flu, which was sweeping across Europe at the time and subsequently died in the No 4 Stationary Hospital at Longuenesse, St Omer.

He was buried in the Longuenesse Cemetery on 11 February by Padre GE Chamberlain. The Padre who succeeded him was the Rev. TW Barker, a Canadian, who wrote to my grandmother; 'We have had so many deaths from influenza here since that I am afraid no one else is likely to remember any particular case.'

My grandfather, Fred, was 41 years old. I have since visited his grave on two occasions with the Hampstead Pals. On his headstone are written the words chosen by my grandmother;

'Thy will be done'

Editor's note:

Longuenesse Souvenir Cemetery

St. Omer is a large town 45 kilometres southeast of Calais and the very name sums up 'HQ of the RFC and RAF during the Great War.' It is also a cracking place to go for a day trip and very useful as a beer break on the alternative route from Calais to Arras, with its many bars and delightful restaurants, thereby avoiding the dull A26 Motorway. The Pals have often taken welcome refreshment in the delightful town centre, where you will find many interesting varieties of Flanders beers. It is also a great place for an overnight stay.

Longuenesse is a suburb of St Omer on the southern outskirts of the town and this large cemetery is approximately 3 kilometres from the town centre beside the busy Wizernes (Abbeville) road. St. Omer was the General Headquarters of the British Expeditionary Force from October 1914 to March 1916. Lord 'Bobs' Roberts, VC, died there in November 1914 from pneumonia aged 82 years. The famous old soldier was a national hero. The town was a large hospital centre during and after the war and most of the graves in this fascinating cemetery are of those who died in the nearby military hospitals, as did Corporal Fred Hine.

St Omer suffered many enemy air raids in November 1917 and May 1918, with serious loss of life. This cemetery, designed by Sir Herbert Baker, has a real 'international flavour' with many graves featuring from the British Commonwealth and beyond. The Commonwealth section of the cemetery contains 2,874 Commonwealth burials of the First World War (6 unidentified), with special memorials commemorating 23 men of the Chinese Labour Corps whose graves could not be exactly located. Second World War burials number 403 (93 unidentified). Within the Commonwealth section, there are also 34 non-war burials, including several graves of Commonwealth War Graves Commission employees and 239 war graves of other nationalities. Nine 'Shot at Dawn' British soldiers are also buried here. The closeness of the large RFC & RAF airfield is testament to the many graves of airmen killed in flying accidents. The site of the airfield is well worth a visit.

During World War I on 8 October 1914, the British Royal Flying Corps (RFC) arrived in Saint-Omer and a headquarters was established at the aerodrome next to the local racecourse. For the following four years, Saint-Omer was a focal point for all RFC operations in the field. Many Royal Air Force squadrons can trace their roots to formation at Saint-Omer during this period.

During World War II, the RAF briefly used the airfield from September 1939 to May 1940. Then, the Luftwaffe arrived and used the airfield. On 9th Aug 1941, the Spitfire of Douglas Bader, the famous British fighter pilot, crashed in the Pas-de-Calais near St Omer. He bailed out, losing one of his prosthetic legs and was captured and taken to the Luftwaffe hospital in the town. While there, his missing leg was returned to him (damaged, but repaired by Luftwaffe engineers), and he was entertained at St Omer airfield officers' mess by the top German ace, Adolf Galland, commander of the JG 27 fighter group. The following night, Bader climbed down a bedsheet rope from the second floor of the hospital and made his escape and was guided by the French Resistance to a safe house some 2km from the airfield. The next morning, he was re-captured and sent to a prison camp in Germany. Following further escape attempts, he was eventually sent to the 'escape-proof' Colditz Castle.

Gunner Francis LOWLES

Lancashire Heavy Battery Royal Garrison Artillery attached
18th Trench Mortar Battery.
Killed in action 27 May 1917
St Martin Calvaire British Cemetery, Nr Arras, France.

Found & commemorated at St Martin Calvaire British Cemetery by grandson Joe
Symon QPM, Detective Chief Superintendent, Merseyside Police (Rtd)

Jon Nicholls writes;

Joe Symon first accompanied the Hampstead Pals in 1999 to the Battlefields of The
Old Western Front. He was great company and was very knowledgeable about the
Great War of 1914-18. He was planning to write a book about the Liverpool & London

Police officers on the Army Reserve and consequently re-called to the colours in August 1914.

He and his son Greg, together with some of his Merseyside Police colleagues, travelled with the Hampstead Pals on four occasions and each time, we would visit Joe's grandfather, Frank Lowles, who is buried in the little cemetery at St Martin Calvaire, which stands on the old 1917 Arras Battlefield at a junction of quiet country lanes. Frank died on 27 May 1917, the day my mother was born.

Tragically, on 19th May 2003, just two days after returning from a Hampstead Pal's battlefield tour, Joe Symon died suddenly.

Greg Symon, his son and ex-Detective Inspector Merseyside Police, writes;

My great-grandfather, Francis Lowles, was a volunteer gunner with the Lancashire Heavy Battery, Royal Garrison Artillery. On the day he was killed, he was in the front line near St Martin attached to a mortar crew of the 18th Trench Mortar Battery. The war diary records that one gunner was killed and two wounded on that day.

Frank was born on 7th August 1891 and was 26 years old when he died. He was a Liverpool docker, living near the docks in an area called Dingle. He married my great-nan, Maggie and they had two daughters, Madge and Bertha - my nan and my dad's mum.

The family were strict Roman Catholics and Nana Bertha was a pupil at St Malachy's Catholic Primary School. She first found out that her dad had died at the school assembly when the headmistress coldly announced that 'Bertha Lowles will be milk monitor today, as her daddy has been killed fighting the Germans.'

Nana was a very religious woman but you could never mention the 'Germans' to her; she had a hatred I have not seen very often. Her mum got remarried to a bloke named Phillip Marlow and had more children. Her half-brother, George Marlow DFM, was killed serving with 51 Squadron Bomber Command on 21st January 1944, when Halifax LV775 was shot down on Ops to Magdeburg. He was 25 five years old and is buried in Berlin War Cemetery.

So, she lost her dad and her brother fighting the Germans and was clearly affected by this throughout her whole life. When I used to visit her every Sunday, you would see her dad's death plaque and her brother's photo in his RAF uniform on the mantelpiece.

I now have Frank's death plaque and medals.

My dad, Joseph Symon, started off as a Liverpool City Police cadet and was a winner of the Kenneth Thomas trophy as the outstanding cadet. He had 32 years of service with numerous commendations. Most of his career was spent in counter-terrorism. He was awarded the QPM and set up the hostage negotiation liaison between the Police and British Special Forces. He travelled the world teaching the same. He went over to France to visit Great-Grandad's grave which was a source of some comfort for Nana, the fact that he had got there before she passed.

Editor's note:

Joe Symon's wish that he would be reunited with his grandfather was carried out by 40 Hampstead Pals on Tuesday 25 November 2003, in company with son Greg, who placed his dad's ashes in Frank Lowles' grave at St Martin Calvaire Cemetery.

The informal but moving ceremony was properly conducted by a local Catholic priest and bagpipes played by fellow police officer, Ian Alexander. The grave was duly anointed with whisky just as Joe would have wished!

St Martin Calvaire British Cemetery can be seen from the main Wancourt – St Martin Road as you enter the village and it stands in quiet fields alongside the French Civilian Cemetery. The village of St. Martin-sur-Cojeul was captured by the 30th Division on the first day of the Battle of Arras on 9 April 1917. It was lost in March 1918 but retaken in the following August. St. Martin Calvaire British Cemetery was named from a wayside calvary that was destroyed during the war. It was begun by units of the 30th Division in April 1917 and used until March 1918. Plot II was made in August and September 1918. This little cemetery, designed by Sir Edwin Lutyens, contains 228 Commonwealth burials of the First World War, five of them unidentified. Frank Lowles, a Liverpudlian, is not alone. He is buried in the company of 42 officers and men of different battalions of the King's Liverpool Regiment, killed in the fighting of 1917-18.

Great-grandson Greg Symon reunites his dad, Joe, with Grandad Frank at St Martin Calvaire British Cemetery, 25 November 2003

Lieutenant Charles POPE VC
11th Battalion Australian Imperial Force
Ex-Metropolitan Police Constable 82 B Division (Chelsea)
Killed in action 15th April 1917
Moeuvres Communal Cemetery Extension

Commemorated at Moeuvres Communal Cemetery Extension by grandson Guy
Nicholson and granddaughter Mary Lotter
'The day my family came'

Jon Nicholls writes;

On Monday 24 May 2014, The Hampstead Pals were accompanied by Charles Pope's
granddaughter, Mary Lotter and his grandson, Guy Nicholson together with his great-

grandchildren and families, to his grave at Moeuvres Communal Cemetery extension. Assistant Commissioner Cressida Dick QPM laid a wreath on behalf of the Metropolitan Police, in which Charles Pope served at Chelsea Division before the Great War.

Also in attendance was the Australian Defence Attaché, Lt Colonel Scott Clingan who laid a wreath on behalf of the people of Australia and read the citation of the VC award. Professor John Grieve CBE, QPM spoke about Charles Pope's service in the Metropolitan Police. We were warmly welcomed to the village of Moeuvres by the Mayor, M. Setan. Also in attendance were Mr Nigel Stevens, representing the Commonwealth War Graves Commission and Mr Mike Jackson representing the London Branch of The Western Front Association.

It was a special day.

Charles Pope was born on 5th March 1883 at 21 Morrison Buildings, Mile End Old Town, East London. His father, William, was a Constable in the City of London Police. Sadly, Charles' mother, Jane, died in 1888 when Charles was five, and his father re-married to Sarah Ann Barkwith in 1897. She was a widow and had three previous children. Charles had four siblings in all. His younger brother, John, would be killed in action in 1918 and commemorated among the missing on the Australian National Memorial at Villers-Bretonneux.

When his mother died, Charles was sent to live with his paternal grandparents at Navestock, Essex, where he attended school. In April 1899, he enlisted in the Royal Marine Artillery, adding a year to his age. He served on HMS Renown from 30th October 1900 to 13th April 1904 and was discharged on 3rd June. He emigrated to Canada soon after leaving the Royal Marines and worked for the Canadian Pacific Railways. He returned to London in 1906 and joined the Chelsea Division of the Metropolitan Police Force on 2 July.

The family gather for the ceremony of remembrance

On 13th December 1906, Charles Pope married Edith Mary Smith at St Luke's Anglican Church, Chelsea, London. He resigned from the Metropolitan Police on 17 December 1910 and emigrated to Australia. They lived at various addresses in Perth, Western Australia and took with them their two children – Edith Maude (born 1907) and Charles William (born 1909). On arrival in Australia, Charles became a furniture salesman for Blain & Co, Perth. He then became an Insurance Agent for the Temperance & General Insurance Co, Perth.

Meanwhile, the war was raging in Europe and Australian forces were heavily engaged on the Gallipoli Peninsula. Consequently, Charles enlisted with the Australian Imperial Force in Perth on 25th August 1915 and was posted to Blackboy Hill, Greenmount, Perth. He was promoted through the ranks to Sergeant and was commissioned to 2nd Lieutenant on 10th February 1916.

On 15th July 1916, he embarked on the transport ship *Ajana* at Fremantle with the 18th Reinforcement Group for the 11th Battalion. He arrived in Plymouth, UK on 1st September and joined the 3rd Training Battalion at Perham Down on Salisbury Plain. He sailed from Southampton for Le Havre on 7th December and was posted to A Company, 11th Battalion on 10th December. He was promoted to full Lieutenant on Boxing Day 1916.

The action for which he was to win a posthumous Victoria Cross occurred on 15th April 1917 near Lagnicourt. Lieutenant Pope was in command of an important picquet post to the east of the village, with orders to hold it at all costs. The enemy, over 2,000 strong, attacked and surrounded the post and ammunition was running short. Lieutenant Pope, in a desperate bid to save the position, was seen to organise a bayonet charge with his men into the enemy force, by which they were overpowered, although heavy losses were inflicted. This gallant officer had obeyed the order to hold out to the last and his body, with those of most of his men, was found in proximity to 80 enemy dead.

Charles had been in France for just four months. He was originally buried where he fell. His body was exhumed after the war and interred in Moeuvres Communal Cemetery Extension, France. The VC was presented to his widow by Sir Ronald Craufurd Munro Ferguson GCMG, Governor-General of Australia, at a parade at Karrakatta Camp, Perth on 23rd November 1917. His medals are now held by the Australian War Memorial, Canberra.

Metropolitan Police Officers of the Hampstead Pals. Mostly retired, some still on the Beat!

Charles was the only officer of the Metropolitan Police to be awarded the VC in the Great War. It is interesting to note that in May 2001, the Commissioner, Sir John Stevens attended the annual commemoration service in France organised by the Hampstead Pals and later by Dame Cressida Dick CBE QPM when she was Assistant Commissioner as shown in the photograph above.

VC Citation (Read by Lt Col. Scott Clingan)

'For most conspicuous bravery and devotion to duty when in command of a very important picquet post in the sector held by his battalion, his orders being to hold this post at all costs. After the picquet post had been heavily attacked, the enemy, in greatly superior numbers, surrounded the post. Lieutenant Pope, finding that he was running short of ammunition, sent back for further supplies. But the situation culminated before it could arrive, and in the hope of saving the position, this very gallant officer was seen to charge with his picquet into a superior force, by which it was overpowered. By his sacrifice, Lieutenant Pope not only inflicted heavy loss on the enemy but obeyed his order to hold the position to the last. His body, together with those of most of his men, was found in close proximity to eighty enemy dead - a sure proof of the gallant resistance which had been made.'

A Policeman's Lot

A fascinating glimpse of the service of PC 82B Charles Pope in 1906, as described by
Deputy Assistant Commissioner John Grieve CBE, QPM.
'I don't care how long he served, he's still one of us!'

If you read the document that a Metropolitan Police clerk wrote about Charles Pope, you would learn that he was born in Barking on 5th March 1883 in the outer reaches of the East End of London in the Borders of Essex. First connection - I worked there. He was a Londoner and Essex boy but *not* a Cockney - you cannot hear Bow Bells there - but you could probably hear a bell that had been made in Mile End Foundry. This is such a bell. However, that would be an injustice because his birth certificate shows quite clearly that he was born at 21 Morrison Buildings, Mile End Old Town. There is a memorial plaque to him in the adjacent square. His birth was registered 5 weeks after he was born. Here is an interesting conundrum and clearly, it does make him a true Cockney. At Mile End, you can hear Bow Bells and probably hear the foundry too. Second connection - I worked there too.

In addition, the birth certificate also tells us one other thing that was new to me. His father, William, was a City of London Police Constable. We do not have time to go into the sometimes difficult relationships between the City Police and the Met., but it leaves a question; how did his father feel when he joined us?

After time spent as a labourer for Canadian Pacific Railroad, leaving in November 1905, he was examined by a surgeon and passed fit on 27th March 1906 and joined the Metropolitan Police on 2nd July 1906. He was 23 years old. He was described as 5'10$\frac{3}{4}$", fair complexion, blue eyes and brown hair. His chest measured 33'[6/10]". In other words, he was tall and slim. He was given the warrant number 93431. He was posted to Chelsea as PC 82 'B'. There is a plaque dedicated to him on the stairway there to this day. (A third connection because I worked there too and walked past it every day). At the time of his attestation, he was shown as living at 39, Canterbury Terrace, Kilburn, NW6.

There was no training school and just minimal classroom work in those days. Essentially, you had to pass a physical and drill test. You had to be semi-literate. Peel

House, the first Training School was set up in 1907 as a result of reform programs. (Instruction Book for the Preparatory Class)

Constable Tom Divall, who joined the Met a few years before, described the recruitment and training process thus:

> "On reporting myself to the Inspector on duty there and giving him my antecedents, he asked me, "Can you fight?" I replied that I could always take my own part when required to do so. His answer was, "That will just do for us." He took me to the Section House and introduced me to the men (sic) of my relief. Dinner was just being served, so I sat down and enjoyed the heartiest meal I had had for many long weeks. In those days, there were no slack hours, no time for learning how to write reports or how to give evidence in Police Courts, but just two hours once a week for one month for certain instructions in police duties. I was simply shown round the beats, day and night, and the rest I had to do on my own responsibility… I found my mates to be as brave as lions, and not one seemed to be afraid of any living being, and they soon put me to the test as to my capabilities. I may tell you I got a good hiding from a burly rough, but nevertheless, I passed my entrance examination and was then one of them. (Divall 1929:11-12)"

As a single man, Charles Pope too would have lived in a Police Section House once a vacancy occurred, possibly at Walton Street in Chelsea in premises the Met owned for many years. He could walk to work from Kilburn.

Chelsea, in the early years of the 20th century, consisted then - as now - of the very rich, living cheek by jowl with the very poor. For policing, I have always thought this was like putting a cage of ravenous lions next door to a butcher's shop selling fillet steak. Charles Pope would have been assigned a 'beat' and a more experienced Constable or Sergeant would explain the route and working methods. The beats are the streets he was marched out to patrol and would have included Kensington Palace, Sloan Square, the big houses on Cheyne Walk where the rich lived and the King's Road with shops, public houses and cafés, but also included World's End, where the poor were. He would have been instructed to salute and say, 'All correct, no reports' to any Inspector or above. This is probably the most misleading police practice instruction ever, as anyone who thinks anything in policing was ever 'all correct,' probably did not know what was actually going on.

Charles Pope would have found himself posted from one extreme to another. In those days on attestation, Constables took three declarations - solemn promises of duty and allegiance: First, a general declaration, second, in respect of policing the Royal Dockyards and third, in respect of security at the Royal Palaces. So, he could be posted to Kensington Palace one day, or another day be dealing with soldiers from the Duke of York's barracks. Then he would, most days, be faced with the perennial policing issues of drunkenness, rowdyism, theft and burglary, violence, domestic and otherwise, prostitution, vice and related issues, football crowds and what was quaintly called, 'aid to town.' Even in my day, 60 years later, that meant public order duties on the next-door division, 'A' then called 'Whitehall' not 'St James' as it is sometimes called today. This 'aid' would include security at ceremonial and political events and crowds.

He was even instructed, 'To walk at a pace of about 2 and a half miles per hour keeping to the outer or kerbside by day with the right hand to the carriageway and walking close to the houses by night.' (I.B.1910:22)

There was, as yet, little motor transport. A horse-drawn van conveyed groups of prisoners while the hand ambulance conveyed drunks or the ill. The Instruction for the Preparatory Class was very specific on how it was to be used:

'The ambulance is to be wheeled from the end nearest the head, with the feet in front, except when ascending a hill or steps, so that the patient's head is always higher than his feet.' (IB 1910:17 (d))

Then there were football crowds. Chelsea Football Club was created at Stamford Bridge in 1905, the first match being played against Hull on 11th September that year and Chelsea won 5-0. It's worth mentioning that Chelsea lost the Khaki Cup Final against Sheffield 3-0 on 23rd April 1915. I wonder if Charles had kept track of the famous team whose crowds the police were learning to control, or was he a West Ham fan from his East End days? Incidentally, entrance to Stamford Bridge cost 6d in those days, with half-price for women. There were, as yet, no women colleagues in the Met. That was to come during the Great War. There were, however, some matrons to deal with women prisoners.

These were the years that contributed to many changes in policing and they resonate with today. Things were similar yet there were many differences.

The communications were rudimentary; a police telegraph system had been introduced in the 1860s and was being slowly upgraded, despite resistance, with the beginnings of a telephone network in Charles' time.

In 1890, the beginnings of a police pension scheme were introduced. The same year, the Metropolitan Police were the first public service to have 'members controlled and contributed' to the Orphans' Fund - an organisation that did massive charitable relief work after the Great War and with precursor elements of the much-maligned Police Federation (always self-improving, though with sometimes questionable decisions by some officials and practices).

The Police Federation itself was not to be formed until after the Police strike of 1919 but the causes were developing. This included, during the period of Charles' career, the Police Union being formed by Inspector John Syme, who was disciplined, sacked and subsequently imprisoned for challenging his senior officers and politicians. There is a mirror image to today, as the admirable, self-improving and pioneering work of the Federation, its parent bodies and their charitable and social work both for their members, their survivors and wider, is largely ignored in a media deluge of political opportunist criticism today - as it was in those days.

Amongst that political agenda of Charles' day, 1908 saw a Royal Commission created by Parliament to examine the policing of street offences including prostitution, soliciting and the very physical nature of policing that I have described, and it questioned the methods of making arrests and physical restraint. The police were very largely exonerated, not least because the character of one important but lying complainant was undermined kindly for us by the French Police.

1909 was the year of the Tottenham outrage and the murder of PC William Tyler by anarchist political fanatics. This period of terrorism would be followed, in 1911, by the siege of Sydney Street and the murder of 3 more officers. All this seems very familiar...

Charles resigned on 17th December 1910, the week before Christmas, for unrecorded reasons. One contribution I might make is that his life timeline and antecedents, as Tom Divall described, could have meant that he increasingly improved his conditions and his education. Constables were encouraged to improve themselves; the earliest book of self-improvement for police in my collection is dated nearly a decade earlier. To be promoted to Sergeant or join the CID, you had to pass the civil service examination. But then I would say that as the Met educated me. So, Charles spent nearly 4 years with us. My experience would be that PCs become effective after about 18 months and increasingly effective thereafter. Charles would have been a useful member of his relief by the time he decided to leave. He certainly knew about

'Earlies, Lates and Nights'. He was clearly remembered and missed, hence the plaque on the stairs at Chelsea.

Mary Lotter (Granddaughter)

The picture we had of our grandfather, Lt Charles Pope VC., took pride of place in our home in South Africa for as long as I can remember. His daughter Edith (my mother), remembered him as a loving father who strongly believed in justice and freedom for all. We are always reminded that he gave his life bravely in battle for these same values.

Tammy Lotter (Great-Granddaughter)

I have always felt close to our great-grandfather, Charles Pope, but this experience with the Hampstead Pals elevated that connection more than I could have anticipated. There was an instant bond with all of those that we met in Arras and I am so pleased that we remain in touch to this day. Sharing deep meaningful conversations and listening to stories from different generations has enriched my life and I am forever humbled and grateful. The level of care and attention to detail with the arrangements were so appreciated, particularly for the ceremony.

If I close my eyes, I can visualise all the faces of those who attended; the men in uniform, the Australian Defence attaché, the beautiful wreaths and candles. The thoughtful and moving hymns and speeches will never be forgotten by our family. It was a life-changing experience and I cannot thank the Hampstead Pals enough for their passion and commitment to the many fallen soldiers. Knowing that Charles Pope has been visited and spoken about with such pride over the years brings us much comfort.

Editor's Note:

Moeuvres is a farming village that lies 6 miles to the west of Cambrai. The sleepy Communal Cemetery Extension can be found on the Inchy Road. Moeuvres remained in German hands during the Battle of Cambrai, 1917, despite three days of desperate attacks by the 36th (Ulster) Division. The village was partly taken by the 57th (West Lancashire) Division on 11th September 1918 and finally cleared by the 52nd (Lowland) Division on the 19th. The villagers had suffered German occupation for the whole of the war until then. The communal cemetery was extended by the Germans between

November 1917 and March 1918. The British Extension was made between September and October 1918 and then expanded after the Armistice when graves were brought in from the nearby battlefields on the Cambrai-Bapaume road, including that of Charles Pope.

The cemetery now contains 565 Commonwealth burials and commemorations of the First World War. 263 of the burials are unidentified. There is a compact mass grave of 93 (mainly Germans) to the left of the cemetery entrance.

Captain Edward Alexander SHEPHERD
4th Battalion, The Black Watch (City of Dundee)
Killed in action 3 September 1916 aged 32
Thiepval Memorial

Found & commemorated at The Thiepval Memorial by granddaughter Jean Latham, who writes;

My grandad, known as 'Ned', was born in Dundee on 25 September 1875, one of twelve children. Son of Walter and Mary Shepherd, Walter was a jute manufacturer with Thompson, Shepherd & Co., Dundee. Ned was the managing director of the company.

He married Alice Jessie Corrie on 18 April 1906 and lived at Brae Cottage, Broughty Ferry, Angus. They had three children; Francis William Shepherd, Philip Reginald Shepherd and Edward Daniel Arthur Shepherd.

It was during the terrible Battle of the Somme when the 4th Battalion Black Watch, of which my grandfather was in 'C' company, took over the narrow frontage between the River Ancre and the Beaucourt Road and attacked enemy positions opposite Hamel with 'A' and 'C' Companies advanced from 'Giant's Causeway' at dawn. The enemy put up a fearsome resistance, however, the objective was reached and German dugouts bombed but support companies were later driven back by the heavy machine-gun fire. The attack was renewed alongside the 11th Royal Sussex and the German support line was eventually reached and held until 4 pm. The battalion was then withdrawn from the line and went back to Englebelmer.

Ned was on leave in Skye with his wife and family when he heard that his Company was having a bad time, so he cut short his leave and immediately went back to France and was killed. Apparently, he was last seen coming out of a sap (short trench) and running towards the German front line. He was initially posted missing and is now commemorated on the Thiepval Memorial to the Missing. I have made the journey to remember him and see his name on several occasions with the Hampstead Pals.

On a personal note, I would like to include part of an interesting letter from Ned in France on 29 February 1916, to his sister-in-law Dorothy Corrie:

Yesterday, some of us made an excursion in the late afternoon to a town near here. We went in by train and had lovely hot baths. Then we went to a large grocer's shop to buy some grub for the mess. As my companions would do nothing but flirt with the good-looking French girls in the shop, we spent a long time there, about an hour and a half and bought a frightful quantity of stuff. We tied it up in three huge packages and went and had dinner. We also had to buy a fowl, for the C.O. is coming to dine with us, but there was no fowl to be had. However, we discovered a huge goose, probably 20 years old and we bought it for 15 Francs. We none of us knew anything about the characteristics of a good or a bad goose, but a very pretty madame in the shop said it was 'garantie' so we took it. Then, of course, laden like tinkers, we missed the last train. We wandered about in the dark and found a motor lorry which had to pass our village. It was full of mail bags and interesting A.S.C. men. Of course, it broke down on the wet dark road and we waited for over an hour for another lorry. Then we transhipped the mail packages and goose (We were very particular about the goose, but I fear its head came off) and got home at midnight. It was great fun, and I hope that bird will prove edible.

Editor's Note:

Ned Shepherd's body was never found and his loss is included among the 9 officers and 210 other ranks who became casualties on 3rd September 1916, a black day for the Black Watch. The day before the attack, the commanding officer of the battalion, Lt Colonel G A McL. Sceales DSO, had issued the battalion with a 'Special order before going into action':

> Before we take an active part in the biggest battle the world has ever seen, I wish all ranks to know that I am more than proud to be in command of such a battalion. I wish I could feel as confident of doing my small part as well as I know all other ranks will be doing theirs. I have a small sprig of white heather given to me by GENERAL HORNBY and sent by SIR DOUGLAS HAIG to bring us luck. I hope it may and I feel that it will; but in any case, I am sure that once more, our native land will have reason to be proud of the 4th Black Watch.

The sprig of white heather did not bring any luck. The attack had ended in failure. It was another valiant but forlorn attempt to advance the line along the hellish Valley of the Ancre. During the night following the attack, another message was sent to the battalion;

> The Army Commander wishes to convey to the 39th Division his sympathy with them in the failure of today's operations. His confidence in them is unabated and he is sure that before long, their bravery and perseverance will carry them to complete victory.

Just another forgotten and sad statistic of the Battle of the Somme which would claim 450,000 British and Commonwealth casualties and 650,000 German by the end of the Battle.

The Thiepval Memorial to The Missing of the Somme

This memorial is described in many guidebooks on the Battle of the Somme. It was designed by Sir Edward Lutyens and unveiled by the Prince of Wales and has been described as 'The greatest executed British work of monumental architecture of the twentieth century.' It certainly marks the height of achievement by the magnificent Commonwealth War Graves Commission. However, being faced in brick means it is constantly being repaired and re-pointed at great cost. It was built between 1928 and 1932 and is the largest Commonwealth Memorial to the Missing in the world. It contains the names of more than 72,000 officers and men of the United Kingdom and South African forces who died in the Somme sector before 20 March 1918 and have no known grave. Over 90% of those commemorated died between July and November 1916. The names of the missing of other Commonwealth countries are contained on their own national memorials. It also serves as an appropriate Anglo-French Battle Memorial in recognition of the joint nature of the 1916 offensive and a small cemetery containing equal numbers of Commonwealth and French graves, brought in from all over the Western Front, lies in garden-landscaped serenity at the foot of the memorial.

The inscription of names on the memorial is reserved for those missing or unidentified; soldiers who have no known grave. A large inscription on an internal surface of the memorial reads:

Here are recorded names of officers and men of the British Armies who fell on the Somme battlefields July 1915 - February 1918 but to whom the fortune of war denied the known and honoured burial given to their comrades in death

On a further sad note;

Jean Latham not only commemorates her grandfather's death in action on the 3 September every year but also that of her father *on the same date.*

Edward 'Ned' Shepherd, who was aged 41 when he died, had left behind a widow and three little sons, the youngest of which, Edward Shepherd, had initially joined his father's old regiment, The Black Watch, before joining the RAF in 1940. During WW2, he had become a night fighter pilot with 29 Squadron, based at RAF Ford West Sussex, flying De Havilland Mosquitos.

On the night of 3rd September 1943, exactly 27 years to the day after the death of his father on the Somme, Edward Shepherd was reported 'Missing' over the English Channel. The Squadron Operations Record Book states;

3.9.43. The Squadron had very bad luck during the night flying of the 3rd/4th losing F/Lt Shepherd and his Nav/Rad F/Sgt Menlove, the latter not long surviving the victory on the 23rd when he flew with Wing Cmdr. Mack. F/Lt Shepherd was a pilot of considerable experience and both were married.

The Glenalmond College Perthshire Book of Remembrance records;

He was a prefect, a member of the XV (Rugby) and Captain of the V111 which won the Ashburton Shield in 1929. In the summer holidays of that year, he was one of the party of six cadets from Glenalmond which went with the Home Cadet contingent to Canada to take part in the annual meeting of the Dominion of Canada Rifle Association at Ottawa. In 1926, he won the Public Schools Fencing Competition (sabres) in London and, in 1927, was a member of the Scottish Schools Fencing Team. In 1930, he was awarded the Buccleuch Medal for Classics and the Carnegie Scholarship and went up to Christchurch, Oxford taking his BA in 1934 and winning the half-blue for fencing. He was a member of the University Small Bore Rifle Club and the University Fencing Club (Sabres). He was commissioned Second Lieutenant 4/5th Black Watch in 1930 (prior to joining the RAF). He was married and had one daughter.

Flight Lt. Edward Daniel Arthur
SHEPHERD
29 Squadron RAF
Killed in action 3 September 1943 aged 32
Commemorated on the Runnymede Memorial, England.

Private Henry James Beckett SHORTER

7th Battalion, The Royal West Kent Regiment
Killed in action 17th July 1917
Perth Cemetery (China Wall), Nr Ypres, Belgium.

Found & commemorated at Perth (China Wall) Cemetery, Zillebeke, by grandson
Alan Shorter, Constable, Metropolitan Police (Rtd), who writes;

My grandfather, Henry Shorter, was born in 1890 and lived at no 15 Hawthorne Grove, Penge. Henry's father was Henry Beckett Shorter, a laundryman of the same address. On the 16th of November 1915, at the age of 25, my grandfather got married to Ethel May Morby, a spinster aged 19 years. They had one son who was my dad, Ronald James Beckett Shorter, who was born 8th of March 1916. During the Second World War, he served in RAF Bomber Command as a Flight Engineer on Lancaster bombers and took part in many bombing raids deep into Germany.

Grandfather Henry joined the 7th Battalion Royal West Kent Regiment in 1915 and served on the Somme and the Battles of Arras and Messines in June 1917.

Because of his untimely death, Ethel had no other children by Henry. He was badly wounded at Zillebeke and he died from his wounds in a casualty clearing station and was later interred at Perth (China Wall) cemetery in July 1919 after his body was recovered from the battlefield. My wife Gilly and I first visited his grave with the Hampstead Pals in 1997.

Editor's Note:

Henry Shorter served with the renowned 18th (Eastern Division) which had fought with distinction on the Somme in 1916. He died from wounds received on the night of 17 July 2017 during a heavy bombardment on the British front line in a trench system known as Ritz Street approximately 200 yards south of the large cemetery where he now rests.

The Battalion War Diary records;

Battalion relieved the 7th Queen's in the front line. Enemy batteries shelled very heavily during the relief. Mustard Oil and Gas shells were also used. Several casualties occurred. 29 Men were (later) sent to hospital suffering from gas poisoning.

Henry's body was buried nearby and later recovered in July 1919 and re-interred in the large Perth (China Wall) Cemetery, which lies on the road halfway between Hellfire Corner and Zillebeke. The cemetery was begun by French troops in November 1914 and was allegedly so named by the 2nd Scottish Rifles who were originally raised in Perth. China Wall was the secondary name given after the great ramparts of sandbags that lined a communication trench, 'The Great Wall of China', nearby. The cemetery now contains 2791 Commonwealth war graves from World War I. Of these, 1369 are unidentified.

It is certainly a strange name for a cemetery. The 'China Wall' apparently derives from the soldier's name for a communication trench that ran from near here north to the Menin Road. The trench would be very shallow due to the height of the water table so sandbags were stacked up above the level of the trench to form a solid rampart and so increase the depth of the trench, hence some called it 'The Great Wall of China'.

China Wall Cemetery 2016. Inset is grandson Alan Shorter who died September 2021

Private John Charles SHULTS

7th Battalion East Surrey Regiment Killed in action 18th
March 1916
Quarry Cemetery Vermelles, Nr Loos, France

Found & commemorated at Quarry Cemetery in 1983 by grandson John Charles
(Jack) SHULTS, Detective Constable Metropolitan Police (Rtd), with Hampstead
Pals and veteran soldiers Bill Hay and Charlie Taylor. Jack writes;

I remember that day in September 1983, when the Hampstead Pals took me for the
first time to visit my grandfather's grave at Quarry Cemetery on the Loos Battlefield.
We were accompanied by two veteran soldiers of the Great War, Irishman Charlie
Taylor and Scotsman Bill Hay. Jon had located the whereabouts of his grave and was

told by the Commonwealth War Graves Commission that my grandad was the only 'Shults' in the British Army! This is because his parents were of German-Dutch heritage and had changed the family name from 'Shultz' to the more English-sounding name of 'Shults' before the war.

My grandad has no family photographs that I know of and my grandma married again and so he was sadly forgotten. My father died at the age of 57 and none of the family spoke of grandad. I still have the East Surrey military history books but they don't help. My brother and I researched as much as we could at Kew and I found one of Grandad's medals and his death plaque when my mother died. I have returned several times to Quarry Cemetery over the years with friends and family.

My grandad was born in Stratford in 1890 and the family moved to 30 Queensbury Street, Islington. When he married my grandma Ellen in 1913, they moved to 14 Robinson Lane, Tooting. He joined the British Army on 24 May 1915 and enlisted at Lambeth Town Hall at the age of 28 years and five months, joining the 7th Battalion East Surrey Regiment. Upon enlistment, he gave his occupation as a 'handyman'.

He arrived with his battalion in France on 30 December 1915 and, just three months later, he was killed in action. I was told he was a company sniper. He had two children; Mary, who died aged 4 months and my dad, also named John Charles Shults. Following the family tradition, my eldest son is also named John Charles Shults, as is his eldest boy, my grandson!

Editor's note:

John Charles Shults was killed during the fierce crater fighting which occurred on 18th March 1916 when, following a heavy artillery bombardment, the enemy launched a determined attack against the craters held by the 12th Division. The 37 Infantry Brigade was holding 'D' Sector the Hohenzollern section of the line and the 7th East Surreys holding the line from Barts Alley to Rifleman Alley, including 1, 2 and 'A' Craters.

Following a deadly bombardment of the Surrey's trenches, the enemy attacked in force and captured much of the Surrey's positions. A counter-attack was launched by the Brigade later that day, which partially proved successful and the line held, although 'A' Crater was lost. Such was the ferocity of the hand-to-hand fighting since being in the front line that the battalion suffered total losses of 330 other ranks plus 8 officers, killed, wounded or missing.

Quarry Cemetery was used from July 1915 to June 1916 and was severely damaged by shell fire, hence John Shults' isolated grave bearing the inscription 'Buried near this spot.' The original grave marker had been overturned by shell fire. This is an interesting and attractive cemetery, 'off the beaten track' and often visited by the Hampstead Pals. It reminds one of a beautiful 'sunken' garden. It is nicely secluded and cannot be seen from the road. It contains a low wall which is perfect for sitting in the sun and eating your baguette while 'toasting the lads' with a glass of vin rouge. Our veteran soldiers certainly found it so, although Bill Hay would demand a *Rusty Nail*.

The cemetery has approximately 140 graves, of which 10 are unknown and contains just 5 of the 7th East Surreys killed during March 1916. It lies up an open track, leading off to the right just before 'Cite Madagascar' or 'Mad Point' on the old 1915 Loos Battlefield.

The quarry in which the cemetery is set was marked on all the trench maps at the time and from the entrance today, the site of the notorious Hohenzollern Redoubt can still be seen. It contains the recently identified grave of the late Queen Mother's brother, Fergus Bowes-Lyon, 7th Battalion, The Black Watch.

The majority of the 7th East Surrey casualties of that fateful 18th March 1916 can be found on the Loos Memorial to the Missing at Dud Corner.

John Charles Shults is also commemorated on the Mitcham war memorial.

You are not forgotten

The Hohenzollern Redoubt in 2015

Private Ernest WOODCOCK

19th Battalion, The Manchester Regiment
Killed in action 31st July 1917
Menin Gate Memorial, Ypres, Belgium

Commemorated at Maple Copse Cemetery by grandson Roger Smith, Detective
Sergeant, Metropolitan Police Flying Squad (Rtd), who writes;

This is the story of an ordinary working man, my grandfather, who became a soldier
in the Great War and lost his life. He won no medals except campaign medals. He is
not remembered as a hero, just a brother, an uncle, a husband, a father, a grandfather
… a soldier who did his duty.

Ernest Woodcock was born in March, Cambridgeshire, in 1890, and was the son of John Tom & Clara Minnie Woodcock. He had 6 brothers and 3 sisters. In the 1911 Census, his occupation was shown as a baker. In 1912, he married Ruth Long, and they had 3 daughters; Gladys Minnie in 1912, Ethel in 1915, and my mum, Olive, on 18th August 1916.

He didn't volunteer but when married men were conscripted, Ernest became a soldier. He trained with the Queen's Royal Regiment West Surrey but served in Flanders with the19th Battalion, Manchester Regiment as Private 51226.

The family photograph was taken outside their cottage and has Olive as a bonny baby on her mother's lap. It was probably Ernest's last home leave. His name is on the War Memorial in my home town, *March,* and when I asked my Mum, 'What happened to him?', she simply said, 'He was missing', and it seems that was all she knew. But the records say he was 'Killed in Action' and I am certain his widow, Ruth, must have been told the official version; she must have known the truth.

That assumption, and the family photograph, inspired me to write a poem that sprang from nowhere but has become a heartfelt tribute not just to the man that my mum and I never knew, but also to the wonderful grandmother I did know;

She never told them, his beloved Ruth. She must have known but she hid the truth from those precious daughters young and good, how their father died in Flanders' mud.

Born in England's eastern Fens and raised amongst hard-working men who tilled the land to keep us fed and raised the corn to make our bread.

Young Ernest had an honest trade, he'd served his time, he'd made the grade. He baked the bread – the staff of life – to earn a wage, support his wife.

He didn't volunteer to fight, he stayed at home and every night he kneaded dough and baked it well, and made loaves for the shop to sell.

I often think he would have thought, that as a Baker, he really ought to have been left on Blighty's shore, to make his bread, and what is more to see his daughters thrive and play, and be there for them every day.

But then the dreaded call-up came, the piece of paper with his name
that told him when and where to go, to learn to fight and kill the foe.

Before they marched him off to war, he posed outside the cottage door
where ivy grew and decked the wall. In uniform he stood so tall.

His daughters at their mother's knee, in Sunday best for all to see -
the photograph records that day, just before he went away.

The family scene so peaceful then, dissolved in horror and agony when
in Flanders' fields, midst rain and gale, he lost his life at Passchendaele.

I don't know how he met his fate; his name's inscribed on the Menin Gate
with many other men so brave who, 'Known Unto God', have no known grave.

And back at home, his widowed wife, consumed by grief at this loss of life,
didn't tell them how their father perished, she protected children that she cherished.

'Missing in action' was all she said, although she knew that he was dead
and that he died in a sea of mud, a hail of bullets, a pool of blood,
a cloud of gas, an exploding shell - caught on barbed wire in a living hell.

Many Great War records were destroyed in the Blitz and nowhere is Ernest mentioned by name, but surviving war diaries of the 19th Manchesters on the day of his death, 31st July 1917, the infamous first day of Passchendaele, describe a scene of horror, carnage and death. No one knows what happened to Ernest; he disappeared. His body was never found, he has no known grave, and his name is inscribed on the Menin Gate at Ypres.

The 19th Manchesters were near Maple Copse, either in the copse itself or in Crab Crawl Tunnel when Zero Hour arrived at 3.50 am. The war diary tells what happened:

'Heavy rain had fallen and the going was dreadfully heavy. Casualties were rather severe. The out-going troops were very much hampered in their movements, exits became choked by wounded men and others trying to return, and they were only able to get out by ones and twos at a time. It was still dark and there was a heavy barrage on the British Front Line.'

It was in that unimaginable chaos that Ernest Woodcock disappeared.

In October 2018, with the Hampstead Pals, my wife and I visited Maple Copse Cemetery and standing quite alone was the grave of an unidentified 'A Soldier of the Great War – Known unto God'. It was there that Celia and I told Ernest's story and laid a wreath to honour that unknown soldier who, most probably, gave his life on the same day during the same attack as my grandfather. Perhaps it is him… and that gave us the closure we needed.

On the grave, we left the Woodcock family photo and another of our granddaughter. The baby on her mother's knee was my mum, born in August 1916, less than a year before her father was killed in July 1917. She was called Olive. In July 2017, almost exactly 100 years after Ernest's death, our first grandchild was born, a gorgeous baby girl also named Olive. That day, we introduced Ernest, if it was him, to his great-great-granddaughter.

Note

Gladys Minnie, known only as Minnie, died from meningitis in 1919, aged 6. Ethel and Olive both lived to a ripe old age. Ruth re-married in 1924 to Bert Cobb who became a loving step-father to Ernest's surviving daughters and was the grandfather I remember. Ruth died, aged 75, in 1959.

RIP Ernest Woodcock.

Roger Smith visits the War Memorial at March in Cambridgeshire in October 2021

Editor's note:

Maple Copse Cemetery was designed by Sir Edward Lutyens and lies to the east of the village of Zillebeke. It was chosen to commemorate Private Ernest Woodcock as, from trench map calculations, it is the nearest burial ground to where he was last seen, the area of the 19th Manchesters' attack being nearby and just to the north of the cemetery.

His name is now commemorated on **The Menin Gate Memorial to the Missing** in Ypres, Sir Reginald Blomfield's triumphal arch, designed in 1921 and completed in

1927. The site was chosen as it was the closest gate of the town to the fighting, and so allied troops would have marched past it on their way to the front. Actually, most troops passed out through the Lille Gate as the Menin Gate was too dangerous due to the constant shellfire. This large Mausoleum of Remembrance contains the names on stone panels of 54,395 Commonwealth soldiers who died in the Salient but whose bodies have never been identified or found. On the panels of the Manchester Regiment, Ernest Woodcock's name can be found. **Maple Copse Cemetery** contains 308 burials and special commemorative headstones of the First World War. Of the 78 burials that could actually be located, only 26 are identified and special memorials commemorate the 230 casualties whose graves in the cemetery had been destroyed by constant shellfire. The name 'Maple Copse' is taken from a small plantation nearby although it gives a homely name to the many Canadian soldiers killed in May & June 1916 and buried here. The place was used by Advanced Dressing Stations and burials took place there both before and after the Battle of Mount Sorrel in June 1916. However, in that engagement and in later fighting, the graves were mostly destroyed.

Photo: Bill Gemmel
The Menin Gate Memorial to the Missing.
'A more sacred place for the British race does not exist in all the world'.
Winston Churchill

CHAPTER 2

As Breezes Remember

Poppy

Red sways in ochre and green
following sun's unwitting smile.
To blush this land with guilt,
so many a far off, lonely heart.

Fed to soils churned from depth,
scars from field to splintered tree.
Here shrapnel flies a breach in time
to pierce grandchild's lonely heart.

As Breezes Remember

Old concrete bunkers crumble,
shocked moments etched in grass.
Listen hard as breezes remember
every stem murmurs a pain of heart.

People missing from families bring generations of regret and loss.
Police Constable Tim Savage, Metropolitan Police.

The Reverend John ASH
Chaplain to the Forces 4th Class
48th Divisional Ammunition Column
Died 7th September 1917
Vlamertinghe New Military Cemetery, Nr Ypres, Belgium.

Found & commemorated at Vlamertinghe New Military Cemetery by great-niece,
Sally Fisher, who writes;

'I hope and pray that I shall be allowed to live' (John's last letter)

On Tuesday 22nd May 2018, whilst on our way to Ypres, the Hampstead Pals stopped
at Vlamertinghe New Military Cemetery where my great-uncle, The Reverend John

Ash is buried. I had long wanted to visit his grave and the opportunity had finally arrived.

John Ash was born on 2ⁿᵈ January 1881 at Matford, near Exeter in Devon, a farmer's son, where the Ash family still live and run the family farm there. Before he became a Chaplain to the Forces, he was Chaplain for the Free Churches at the Red Cross Hospital, Northwood House, Cowes, Isle of Wight. He was married to Mary and lived at 'Vailima', Newport Road, Cowes, Isle of Wight. They had no children.

He was ordained as a Methodist Minister and became a Chaplain to the Forces on 16 January 1917, initially attached to the 1st Battalion, The Queen's (West Surrey) Regiment 33rd Division and then to the 48th (South Midland) Divisional Ammunition Column.

He was killed instantly by a German bomb dropped from an aeroplane whilst in his billet near Vlamertinghe, during the night of 7th September 1917, while the Battle of Passchendaele was at its height. The same bomb wounded the Colonel and four other brother officers, one of whom died the next day.

John was 37 years old and an Army Chaplain 4th Class, which meant he held the rank of Captain although was always addressed as 'Padre'. He was buried the following day in the presence of 200 men who it was said, 'felt his death keenly' as he had always been so helpful to the men in his division.

It was a beautifully sunny day when we held our commemoration for Great-Uncle John and moving extracts from several letters that he wrote to his wife and family were read out, including one that was written on the day he died, in which it seemed as if he sensed that his days were numbered as he asked his family to care for his wife should he be killed. John Grieve then read a poem, 'The Day My Family Came', which was particularly relevant and moving. The last verse of this is quoted here (with kind permission of poet Michael Edwards). The short commemoration was concluded with the Pals in their typical fashion, raising glasses of champagne to Padre Ash, which no doubt would have brought a wry smile to his face, as he was a Methodist Minister!

Now I am at peace and free to roam
Where 'ere my family speak my name,
That day my soul was called back home
For on that day my family came.

1st Queen's

33rd Division

24-4-1917

Dear Tom and Flo

I am glad to say I am safe while others about me are now dead. I rose yesterday at 6 am and was doing all I could with the doctors up to sunset. When I returned, I was completely finished. I cried and went to sleep. To see a modern battle is simply awful. I was among my men all day on Sunday and where, I must not tell you, as it is against military law and I am censored too, so I must not break the law. The fighting now is terrible; the big guns are so awful that you cannot at times endure it. The German prisoners look like dead men when they are brought out of the trenches. The Germans are a cruel lot; all the villages - and all the small fruit trees are all cut to the roots. Our men have no cover now when advancing, and yet we kept them back. The weather is lovely now and I should hope it is with you; I know how badly you need it.

You will be glad to know my wee sweet wife is anxious to see me. I cannot leave without first getting a chaplain to serve in my place. You may guess how important is such work now. I wish you could see these brute flies; we get such big ones. I am sending back tomorrow for some stuff to kill them. As the summer comes, they will breed all the more quickly.

Well, I hope you are all well. How peaceful to go to bed in assurances that no shell can drop on you. I am very glad to hear that Dad is coming out to live with you. I have been telling him it is the right thing to do. I will write to him again soon, but I am very busy now as you will understand. Tell all the family to write to me when they have time, and as it takes a long time to reach me, only a good cake or any dried fruit will keep in good condition. We were on biscuits for 10 days; they are like wood to eat. I will close now.

Love to all. Thousand times thank you.

Good Morning

John

1st Queen's Regiment

B.E.F.

Sunday Evening

Dear Father

I am very well and happy in my work and will be when I get to know all my work. The officers are all so kind to me. The Commander comes in to see me and wishes me goodnight always. I was reading my Bible when he came the other evening, and he said, 'I will try and not swear in your presence tomorrow, chaplain'.

I sleep on straw when I can get it, if not, on the boards, they are so hard. The cold is awful, the water becomes ice on your face when you are washing if you are not quick to the towel at work. I have never felt the cold like it. The poor Tommy in the line all the night watching for the hun, cold and yet brave and full of cheer. I saw some coming back yesterday. I had to take them to camp; I cried as I walked in front of them and gave the orders; I am sure the men saw I was crying. I made the cooks give them all a special tea (but they are brave). Funerals are conducted at night near the line. The different commanding officers know where to send for me, then I go with the guide, he takes me to the graveyard. I take the things in his pockets, his number and name, and write to his people and report to the senior chaplain. I also put up a small cross and write on it.

You never thought that a son of yours would ever experience war like this, did you? I know you will pray for me, tell God to take care of me. I am in danger of being shot at any time, as are all who are near the line. When you see Annie, William, Tom, Edith and Mary, tell them to remember me every night. I wish you could all meet as a family and pray that 'one prayer' together that God will save my life. I want to live too for my dear wife's sake; she was so brave when the time came for me to leave. Can you read this awful scribble, Dad? How are you? Tell me all about yourself when you write. Is it cold in England?

We passed through a village yesterday, not one stone left upon another; the church is level with the ground, the graves torn to pieces. War is awful.

Goodbye

All my love

John

John's last letter to his brother. Written on the day he was killed, from a dugout near Vlamertinghe, Ypres.

48th Division

D.A.C.   R.F.H.

7-9-1917

Dear Tom and Flo

I am deeply sorry to learn of your accident. I hope you are now in your normal again, as I know what it must mean for you to be laid aside just now. You are getting fine weather as we are out here; this will mean so much to your respecting your corn.

Mary, as you know, is at Spreyton with Annie; she will come to Bridestowe and stay with you as you think best, you make your own arrangements about that. She is no trouble as you know.

I am here with my life in my hands. She does not know of my dangerous position. I cannot tell her, she would grieve so, God only knows we may be blown to pieces at any moment. We are being bombed, shelled and gassed every night. This is the most terrible part of the whole line. So, between you, my dears, see to my poor wife.

I am not concerned about myself in case I get killed; my one worry is what about my poor wife. The real reason for sending Mary to Devon is that I do not want her to be alone in case I get a knockout blow. At Cowes, she sleeps all alone, now she is in company. I hope I shall come through for her sake. You can show this to Edith, William and poor old Father when you see him.

If I do get killed, I know you will be just to my poor wife. But I hope and pray that I shall be allowed to live. I must keep my present dangerous position from you all, or it would come as a terrible shock. I am now going up again.

Love to all

John XXX

1/3 South Midland
Field Ambulance
Sep 8th 1917
Dear Mrs Ash
I am grieved to have to tell you that your husband Rev John Ash was killed last night at 11.30 by a German bomb. They had retired to rest but aroused by the first bomb which fell, was about to take shelter in a trench nearby, when the second caught him. He was killed instantly and the same bomb wounded the Colonel and four of his brother officers. We laid his body to rest today in the presence of the officers and two hundred men. I shall write to you by next post and give you fuller details as just now I am called away to another part of the division.
With deep sympathy.
Yours very sincerely
H. Arthur Meek S.C.7 (Senior Chaplain)

Sept 9th 1917
1/3rd South Midland
Field Ambulance
Dear Mrs Ash
I promised to give you more details of the funeral of your dear husband. He was very fond of a team of six magnificent mules in the ammunition column. They, therefore, turned them out to draw the GS wagon which bore his body. About 200 men were drawn up in two ranks facing each other, resting on their arms reverently, then non-commissioned officers acted as pallbearers and bore the body between these lines before placing it on the wagon. A procession was then formed. First, the Firing party which acted as an advanced guard marching with arms reversed, then the team and wagon and officers marching on either side. Finally, the main body of the men.

At the cemetery 2 miles from the unit, again the body was borne between the open ranks before I met it and led the way to the grave. We all gathered round and at the close of the service, a salute was fired and the 'last post' sounded on trumpets which transport units have instead of bugles.

This morning, I took the service which Mr Ash had arranged with the D.A.C. We used his hymn books and I allowed the men to keep them at the close of the service, in memory of their Padre. I also distributed the little testaments that he had sent out for them. The officers and men felt his death keenly, for he was with the unit long enough for them to learn to love him. He was absolutely out to help his men and they soon learned to know it. Your husband's personal possessions will be sent to you by the unit through the army agents.

I feel how futile it is for me to try and express sympathy, but as one who has lost three brothers and my own little girl niece since this dreadful war began, I can enter a little into your sorrow.

H. Arthur Meek S.C.F. Non-C.E.

Editor's note:

The Rev. John Ash is one of two Army Chaplains buried in Vlamertinghe New Military Cemetery. The Rev. William Geare aged 26, who lived at 14 Chalcot Gardens, Hampstead, was serving with the 7th and 9th King's Liverpool Regiments, when he was killed whilst tending to a wounded man on 31st July 1917, the opening day of the Battle of Passchendaele.

At the start of the Great War, there were only117 'Chaplains to the Forces' serving in the British Army. That number would rise to 3,475 by 1918, 60 per cent of whom were Anglican, 25 per cent Catholic and 15 per cent of other denominations and faiths, which would include Methodist Chaplains. All were volunteers and a total of 172 would lay down their lives, a higher proportion of officers killed than in any other section of the Army. Three were awarded the Victoria Cross.

Tubby Clayton, the illustrious and famous soldier-priest whose war experiences encouraged the formation of 'Toc H' wrote;

'They were true priests, true men. The Church scarce knew she held them. Their names are now forgotten but many men's hands welcomed them into paradise.'

Vlamertinghe New Military Cemetery is often visited by the Hampstead Pals and many a glass of malt whisky has been raised at the graveside of legendary soldier, **Sergeant John Skinner, VC, DSM & Bar, MM** of 1st Battalion King's Own Scottish Borderers. The cemetery is located five km west of Ieper town centre and to the south of the village of Vlamertinge. The Pals brought Company Sergeant Major Bill Hay of the 9th Royal Scots here in 1982 to 'Drink with a fellow Sergeant and Jock'.

For much of the First World War, Vlamertinghe (now Vlamertinge) was just outside the normal range of German shell fire and the village was used both by artillery units and field ambulances. Burials were made in the original Military Cemetery until June 1917, when the New Military Cemetery was begun in anticipation of the Allied offensive launched on this part of the front in July. Although the cemetery continued in use until October 1918, most of the burials are from July to December 1917. The cemetery now contains 1,813 Commonwealth burials of the First World War.

Rifleman Reginald Percy BARRELL

21St Battalion, The King's Royal Rifle Corps
Attached. 41st Machine Gun Company
Died of Wounds received in action 26 March 1918
St Hilaire Cemetery, Frevent, France

Found & commemorated at St Hilaire Cemetery by family friends Helen & Roger
Learney, Constable, Metropolitan Police (Rtd). Helen writes;

My friend, Carole Evans from Cheam, had asked me if we could visit her uncle Reggie
on her behalf, on one of our Hampstead Pals battlefield trips. This had been mooted
a couple of years before, and so our long-awaited visit finally took place on Sunday 24th
May 2015. As far as we know, we were the first people to visit his grave.

Reginald Percy Barrell, better known as 'Reggie', was born in 1896, in Nettlestead, Baylham, Suffolk, the son of Edmund Archer Barrell and his wife Annie; one of 11 children, 9 of whom survived childhood. He worked as a farm labourer before coming to London, staying with his older brother, Edmund Archer Barrell. In due course, Reggie enlisted in the army in Camberwell. He joined the 21st Battalion of the King's Royal Rifle Corps. There is a photograph taken at Aldershot in 1916 where I believe he trained, and he was posted to Italy in November 1917 for a while before returning to France in early March 1918. He was the great uncle of my friend Carole, and the uncle of Hilda Barrell, who also plays a significant part in this story. Hilda was the older sister of Carole's mother, who was born the day after The Great War ended, 12th November 1918. On the 17th March 1918, young Hilda had written to her uncle Reggie. It is such a sweet letter and finishes with her love and many kisses. It never reached her beloved uncle and was subsequently returned to Hilda.

The original envelope shows that the letter had initially been sent to Italy where the battalion had been posted in November 1917 and by the time it reached France, Reggie had died. We can only imagine the impact that the loss of this young man had on the Barrell family.

I read Hilda's letter out to Uncle Reggie at his graveside, along with a brief outline of Uncle Reggie's personal and family life. This was a very poignant moment and so moving, to read a letter from nearly 100 years before to a young man who gave his life. He was a much-loved member of the family who had clearly made an impact on his niece. In those few minutes, I really felt that Reggie could hear Hilda's words through me…

211 Southampton Street
Camberwell . S.E
17. 3. 18

My Dear Uncle Reggie,
              Just a few lines in answer to
you most welcomed letters we received them both dated
March 12: 1918. We are very sorry to hear about
your Battalion being cut up. We are glad to hear
you keeping well as it leaves us the same. We are
send" You a pound and mama will send you a parcel
Well Uncle I have gone up into the seventh standered
the highest class in the school. Dada is on night
duty so mama and me are alone as dada dordose not
come home till half past one in the morning. Auntie
Alice has to go in the hospital again. We hear that
Grandfather is quite well. Uncle Alf is still in France
We have had the tank come to our borrow borough
opposite the Townhall it was there for two days.
Well Dear Uncle it seems along time since we have
seen you we wish you ment it that you was
going to have a leave. Dada has to shut the
shop all day Monday and one oclock Thursday
we are very busy with the cissors cutting off the
little cupons. Now I must close as I have not much
to say this time. Mama and Dada sent their love
xxx xxxxx x xx Love and xxx xx xxx xxxx xxxxxxx
ixx xxxx xx x xx from xxxxxxxxxxxxxxx
                    Hilda xxxxxxxxxx xx xxx

76

Roger Learney writes;

> *I have tried to throw some light on what actually happened to Reggie. As Hilda mentions in her letter to him, she is sorry to hear about the break-up of his battalion. The 21st Bn KRRC was apparently disbanded on 16th March; this is confirmed by a number of sources.*

> *Some extracts are shown here from the war diary of the 41st Machine Gun Company*

> **17 March 1918**. *On this day the 41st Battalion Machine Gun Corps was formed. The Companies concentrated in billets at Sombrin. The Company was made up to strength with men from disbanded Infantry battalions. (Editor's italics).*

> **21 March** *The battalion was divided into various groups, personnel moving by train and transport by road at different times. The destination was altered and it became apparent that the battalion was going to take part in operations. HQ, B & D Coys, detrained at Achiet-le-Grand and settled for the night in Berkley Camp, Bihucourt.*

> **22 March** *A & C Coys detrained at Achiet-le-Grand and proceeded to Favreuil. 'A' Company went in the line before Beugnatre and no 2 section 'C' Coy reinforced 25th MG bn. 'B' Coy relieved guns of the 6th MG Bn north of Bapaume. 'D' Coy in Divisional reserve at Bihucourt.*

> **23 March**. *Enemy attacked at 2 pm and was repulsed after 3 hours of fighting.*

> **24 March**. *Enemy again attacked on the whole front. No 2 sec 'A' coy retired after covering infantry retirement through Fremicourt across the Bapaume Road to the high ground in rear of Fremicourt. The right continued to fall back, and, conforming to the movement of the above section, fell back into Bapaume finally making a stand on a line to the west of Bapaume, running in front of Grevillers. Nos 1 & 2 Sec 'A' coy resisted the attack until 7.30 pm when, Beugny being captured and Beugnatre having been evacuated, withdrew to high ground north of Favreuil on the right a line was established in front of Biefvillers, 'D' company retired on Favreuil and thence to a line SE of Sapignies eventually taking up positions around Bihucourt under orders of the 122 Inf Brigade. C & B Coys retired to the Biefvillers line and eventually established themselves in a trench S of Bihucourt*

25 March. The enemy advanced in the afternoon but was repulsed by our rifle and MG fire. All the existing guns of the battalion were now in the trench SW of Bihucourt under the command of Col Beal. Resistance was maintained until midnight.

The diary further records that orders were received to 'retire' at 1 am on the 26th of March. So, somewhere in the early part of that very fierce and confused fighting, Uncle Reggie was wounded and most probably evacuated by rail or road the 30 miles from Achiet-le-Grand to Frevent.

Interestingly, I have found that Lance Corporal Peter Fred Beresford, who is shown as 21Bn KRRC, is also buried at Frevent, although no supplementary unit is shown on his record. He died on 30th March. Lt Richard Williams, who is buried at Gezaincourt, died on 2nd April; he is shown as 41 Company Machine Gun Corps. I think that there is little doubt that they were also wounded at about the same time. It gives some idea of the confusion involving these units and their personnel. It's just about the worst way to get involved in what was desperate fighting.

Editor's note:

Frevent was an important town behind the main battle zone and on the lines of communication during the First World War. The 43rd Casualty Clearing Station was posted there from April to June 1916, part of the Lucknow Casualty Clearing Station in June, the 6th Stationary Hospital from June 1916 to the end of August 1918, and the 3rd Canadian, 19th and 43rd Casualty Clearing Stations in the summer of 1918. The great majority of the burials in the cemetery were carried out from these hospitals. St. Hilaire Cemetery Extension was used from March to August 1918 during the 'Kaiser's Battle' (German Offensive) in which Reggie Barrell was mortally wounded.

The cemetery now contains 210 Commonwealth burials of the First World War. There are also 12 Second World War burials, all dating from late May to early June 1940 and the withdrawal of the British Expeditionary Force ahead of the German advance.

The 21st (Service) Battalion (Yeoman Rifles) was formed in September 1915 from volunteers from the farming communities of Yorkshire, Northumberland and Durham by orders of Northern Command. The new battalion moved to Duncombe Park at Helmsley. The family home of the redoubtable Earl of Feversham, (later killed at Flers) and Member of Parliament who took personal command of the raising of the battalion.

In January 1916, the battalion moved to Aldershot and came under orders of the 124th Brigade in the 41st Division, and, on 4th May 1916, it arrived in France. The battalion took an active part in the Battle of the Somme where it was heavily engaged in the advance from Flers to Guedecourt suffering many casualties. In November 1917, the battalion moved with the Division to Italy but returned to France in early March 1918 when it was disbanded.

The Hampstead Pals have, on several occasions, visited the grave of Charles Duncombe, Earl of Feversham, who rests in the AIF Burial Ground (Green Lanes), Flers. He was killed leading his battalion into action on 15 September 1916 at the Battle of the Somme and his body was later found by his adjutant, Anthony Eden, a future Prime Minister and later Lord Avon.

Private Charles BIDDLE
1st Battalion, The Hampshire Regiment
Died of Wounds 28th April 1916
Foncquevillers Military Cemetery, France

Found & commemorated at Foncquevillers Military Cemetery by niece, Jacqui
Downing and great-niece, Caroline Carr.
'Where Have All The Flowers Gone?'
Performed by Sergeant Bernard Williams, Metropolitan Police (Rtd). Caroline writes;

Charles Biddle was born to Joseph and Kate Biddle of 27 Clinton Street, Winson
Green, Birmingham. The family lived in a tiny terraced house not far from the prison.

There was Jo, Charlie, Gert, Kate, Dora, Clarence and Jack. (Dora was Mum's mother – my grandmother)

Charlie was his mother's 'favourite' and she would save all the best food for him. The limited family stories of him are minor but based on acts of sensitive kindness culminating in his lovable nature. He was engaged to 'Joan' who was bereft following his death. She later married someone else but would still get upset over Charlie when speaking with the family.

The war diary of the 1st Hampshires says;

> 'We had very bad luck on the afternoon of the 28th. A small working party was in the fire trench at a point where a communication trench runs into it. By the greatest fluke, the Germans dropped a 5.9" shell straight into the trench at this point killing four and wounding three.'

We can only surmise that Uncle Charlie was one of the working party and subsequently died of his wounds. Sadly, there are limited family stories of him as he died aged 20 years and no photos of him survive in this side of the family. However, his sensitive kind nature has shone through the decades. At the time of his death, Charlie should have been at home on leave, but he gave his leave to a friend who had just become a father… Consequently, the inscription on his grave is very fitting;

A loving Son

A brother kind

Beautiful memories

Left behind

Afterwards, the friend braved a visit to Charlie's mother and told her that Charlie had said to him, 'You go home and see your new baby.' We are not sure how Gran responded because, on hearing of the death of her favourite son, she went into shock. She sat by the fire for two weeks and wouldn't speak to anyone. It was thought the shock brought on her diabetes!

Editor's note(s):

Charlie Biddle now rests in Foncquevillers Military Cemetery, together with his three mates of that fateful afternoon's working party, who were all killed by that German

'Five-Nine', a lethal howitzer shell. Robert Graves in his classic book, 'Goodbye To All That' says, 'five-nines were called 'Jack Johnsons' because of their black smoke.' This was a reference to the first black heavyweight world champion boxer, Jack Johnson (World Heavyweight Champion 1908-1915).

Ironically, Charlie's friend, Private **James Thomas Leech** aged 20, also a 'Birmingham lad' of 140 Crockett's Road, Handsworth, lies close to him. It appears that these four soldiers were all buried in the same grave. His headstone bears the following inscription;

Rest In The Lord The Victory Won.
Mother & Country Say Well Done.

Another of the four killed was Private **Fred Wilson** aged 18, a 'London lad.' The other young soldier killed was Private **Harry Iveny** aged 23. (No details are known)

Foncquevillers Military Cemetery

This peaceful and tranquil cemetery, often visited by the Hampstead Pals, was started by French troops when they held the line here in 1915.

The Allied front line then ran between the villages of Foncquevillers and the enemy-held village of Gommecourt. Both villages were totally destroyed during the war. The whole area was taken over in September 1915 by the British Army which, consequently, used the cemetery and it remained in use until March 1917. The burials in July 1916 are especially numerous. The cemetery was used again from March to August 1918 when the great German March offensive brought the front line back to almost the original position. Seventy-four graves were brought in from the battlefield after the Armistice and the 325 French military graves were removed to the huge La Targette French National Cemetery near Arras.

The cemetery contains 648 Commonwealth burials of the First World War. 53 of the burials are unidentified but there are special memorials to two casualties known to be buried among them. There are five Canadian airmen of the Second World War buried in the cemetery, all killed when their Halifax Bomber of 427 Squadron, based at Leeming, North Yorkshire, was shot down during a raid on Arras Railway Station on 13 June 1944. There are also four Germans and one French non-World War burial. The cemetery was designed by **Sir Reginald Blomfield**.

This village lay just behind the British front line and was the home of the 46th (North Midland) Division for nearly a year. It was a hotspot, and, according to Bill

Partridge, more often known as 'Funky Funking Villas' (or worse) to the British troops. After the war, the village was adopted by the town of Derby in memory of many of its sons who were billeted and buried there.

In the **Foncquevillers Military Cemetery** are buried many of the men of the 46th (North Midland) Division who were killed while that Division held this sector, including those killed on the 1st July and whose bodies were recovered from the German wire and No Man's Land when the Germans retreated in March 1917. Among them is the grave of **Capt. John Leslie Green, VC, RAMC** and Sherwood Foresters. Although wounded, he went to the assistance of an officer hanging on the wire and dragged him back almost to safety when he was killed by rifle fire.

An interesting grave is that of **Lt Col. C.F.G Humphries** whose headstone records an impressive set of decorations - DSO, MC and bar, and DCM earned in an unusual war record. This New Zealand soldier did not serve with his own country's units but, starting as a private, served in the Army Service Corps, the Manchester Regiment, the Highland Light Infantry, the Duke of Cornwall's Light Infantry and Labour Corps (probably while recovering from wounds) and finally commanding the 1st Norfolks with whom he was killed in August 1918 when he was hit by shell fire in an attack on the village of Achiet-le-Petit. His adjutant, Captain G.C. Tyler, was also killed and occupies the next grave.

Another interesting grave is in row C of plot 2, near the top right-hand corner of the cemetery; that of Private Thomas Palmer of the 1/4 Leicesters, killed in February 1917. One of his parents chose this heartrending inscription on his grave;

Will some kind hand in a foreign land place a flower on my son's grave.

Note

Caroline and her mum, Jacqui, have journeyed to the battlefields on many occasions with the Hampstead Pals. They are ordinary people from a Birmingham family torn apart by war. During WW2, the family suffered another grievous loss. Although written about elsewhere, we are proud to record Caroline's personal, 'Fragment of Remembrance' from another terrible war to her 'Uncle Bill'....

Able Seaman William Alfred Savage VC

Royal Navy. H.M.M.G.B 314
Killed in Action 28th March 1942, St Nazaire.
Falmouth Cemetery, Cornwall, UK.

Commemorated by niece Jacqui Downing and great-niece Caroline Carr, who writes;

My Uncle Bill, Able Seaman William Alfred Savage VC – Smethwick's most famous son - was born on the 30th October 1912 to James and Catherine Savage. He was the youngest and last child. His mother had 22 pregnancies of which seven survived to adulthood. They all lived in a tiny two-up and two-down terraced house in Raglan Avenue, Smethwick. Bill attended school locally and, like his father and brothers, found work at M & B's Cape Hill Brewery on leaving school aged 14 years.

The Savage family (male members in particular) were streetwise, lovable roughs. They loved a drink, shared a sense of humour and were the life and soul of any party gathering on a Saturday night. Bill was quieter than his older brothers. He was more sensitive and possessed a strong sense of right and wrong. He was popular at the brewery, being secretary of the bottling store's darts club, a member of the swimming team and a keen water polo player. He could lift a barrel of beer over his head, all physical skills that would be called on during that fateful night in 1942. He married his childhood sweetheart Doris in 1936 and set up home in Durban Road which was within spitting distance of Raglan Avenue, his old school and the Brewery.

At the outbreak of the war, he and his brother Jack signed up for the Royal Navy. Bill was posted to Chatham and commenced a gunnery training course. Following this, he served in Coastal Defence Forces. Bill was then assigned to the brand new MGB 314 as a pom-pom gunner. The 314 regularly worked out of Dartmouth and often sailed to Falmouth, their mission being to land and pick up agents on the French coast. (All in the days before agents were dropped in by Lysander and I'm sure there was a trip to Norway at one point. Also, I'm under the impression that information had been bought back from France on one of these sorties regarding the St Nazaire Raid.)

Their work was often dangerous, sailing in bad weather or by full moon and landing on treacherous shores; places the Germans would least expect. Due to the nature of his work, Bill was granted leave between his missions and was often teased by some family members for being a 'weekend sailor' and if asked, he would say, 'It's only work.' His wife and family had no idea of what he did at this time until after his death.

Motor Gun Boat 314 was soon assigned to a special combined operations mission, the target being Europe's largest dry dock at St Nazaire. The Normandie Dock was highly prized by the Germans as it was big enough to facilitate their Pocket Battleship Tirpitz, for repairs. (Her sister ship, Bismarck, had been sunk by this time).

At this point in the war, there was little good news or the likelihood of any. The Admiralty had, for some time, been looking for a way to destroy this instillation and at the start of 1942, devised an ingenious and daring plan to send a task force of MLs, MTBs and MGBs up the Loire Estuary led by a destroyer whose bows were packed with tons of explosives. The destroyer would then ram the Caisson (gate) of the dry dock and the delayed charges, when exploded, would destroy the Caisson and render the dock tidal, thus denying the Germans its use for the remainder of the war. Each vessel would carry parties of Commandos who were tasked with the demolition of certain port installations. All vessels were modified to complete the journey by sea and cope with the sandbanks of the Loire Estuary.

During these preparations, Bill had injured his leg when jumping onto a stage and appeared to pull a muscle. He was unable to work. The captain of 314 decided to get a replacement. After a few days, he seemed to recover and was determined to be back on duty. Bill's replacement gunner, A.R. Stephens, was retained and they both went on the raid. They were the only members of MGB 314 crew to be killed. Leave was granted prior to the raid. Each and every man knew it was a one-way trip and if anyone felt themselves unable to go, they could stand down. No one did. Bill knew the odds.

On 26 March, the flotilla sailed from Falmouth. As the convoy entered the Estuary, MGB 314 would sail ahead of the destroyer HMS Campbeltown to guide the way in. Exposed by coastal searchlights, signals were sent to the Germans to buy time as they made their way towards the dry dock. Unable to keep up the ruse, the White Ensign was raised and 'all hell was let loose'.

The task force came under merciless fire. On the approach, MGB 314 came under attack by an anchored Sperrbrecher (German Minesweeper). Bill set to work with his pom-pom and spraying the Sperrbrecher from end to end. He silenced every gun.

Once the Caisson was in sight, MGB 314 swerved out of the way enabling the Campbeltown to ram the dock gates. By now all the MLs were under heavy fire which deterred, to a degree, the Commando parties about to be landed.

Bill, with his gun-layer Frank Smith at the forward pop-pom, displayed inspirational courage and skill. Fully exposed without shield to enemy fire from all sides, Bill silenced a pillbox on the Old Mole by sending several shells through the embrasure thus silencing all guns. Moments later, the position was re-manned by the enemy and again, Bill accurately fired his shells through the slit silencing the guns for a second time. It was a remarkable feat of gunnery, bearing in mind he was firing from a pitching and moving platform. He continued to engage the defences, shooting at difficult skyline targets beyond the U-Boat basin and putting out troublesome shoreline searchlights.

Surrounded by damage and devastation and with nothing else to achieve, the order was finally given to withdraw and head for home. It was around this time and on the way out of the dock that Bill was hit and killed.

Profoundly sad. He was killed on his fifth wedding anniversary.

On reaching open sea, MGB 314 rendezvoused with HMS's Atherstone and Tynedale and the wounded were transferred. MGB 314 was deemed to be so badly damaged that it was scuttled. Bill was brought back to Falmouth where he was buried. He was posthumously awarded the Victoria Cross.

Citation London Gazette; 21st May 1942

For great gallantry, skill and devotion to duty as gun layer of the pom-pom in a Motor Gun Boat in the St Nazaire Raid. Completely exposed and under heavy fire, he engaged positions ashore with cool and steady accuracy. On the way out of the harbour, he kept up the same vigorous and accurate fire against the attacking ships until he was killed at his gun.

This Victoria Cross is awarded in recognition not only of the gallantry and devotion to duty of Able Seaman Savage but also of the valour shown by many others, unnamed in Motor Launches, Motor Gun Boats and Motor Torpedo Boats, who gallantly carried out their duty in entirely exposed positions against enemy fire at very close range.

The heavily defended port of St Nazaire was destroyed when fighting off enemy German fire, the men managed to blow up the old destroyer HMS Campbeltown, which had been packed with explosives and disguised as a German ship. The Dock was put out of action for the rest of the war.

Operation Chariot on March 28, 1942, led to the deaths of 168 of the 622 men who left Falmouth and the capture of many more. It also resulted in 89 decorations being awarded for the raid, including five Victoria Crosses.

At the time, *Earl Mountbatten of Burma* said, "Surely, by far, the highest number of VCs ever awarded for a single operation, and this is the measure of the heroism of all who took part in that magnificent enterprise."

Before they set off, the men had been told by their commander that the job was dangerous and he didn't expect anyone to return. Therefore, he didn't want anyone married or with family responsibilities to go and anyone who felt they could not go was given the option to stand down.

Off the record, I would say that Uncle Bill's best friend and crewmate was Billy Banister. If it wasn't for him, Bill's body would have been buried at sea and not brought back home. Apparently, Uncle Bill (apart from his wound) did not look as if he had a scratch on him. They did up his duffle coat after he had been taken down into the wardroom and hatched a plan. They strapped him to a ladder as they rendezvoused with HMS's Atherstone and Tynedale, who were taking the wounded. They pretended he was a casualty and that's why he was brought back to Falmouth.

Editor's note:

Falmouth became a 'drifter' base during World War One; in January 1915 and in 1918, it was a centre for ship repairs. 'Drifters' were fishing trawlers converted to carry a small crew and a six-pounder gun, a forerunner of the MGB of the Second World War as manned by Bill Savage and his crew.

Falmouth Cemetery contains 87 First World War burials, including those of two unidentified firemen from the S.S. "Clan Cumming", attacked by a German submarine in the English Channel on 5 November 1917, with the loss of 13 lives.

During the Second World War, Falmouth was a significant naval base and Royal Navy Air Station. The town was also bombed by the Germans and 31 townsfolk were killed. There was also a military hospital in the town. A war graves plot contains 74 of the 111 Second World War burials within Falmouth Cemetery; the rest are scattered.

In 2018, on the 76th anniversary of the fateful raid, a Commemoration service was held on The Prince of Wales Pier at the stone memorial to the raid. The mayor of Falmouth remarked;

The men left from Falmouth and came back to Falmouth. Being involved in minor skirmishes in the navy myself, I know there wasn't much chance of any of them coming back.
Therefore, he didn't want anyone married or with family responsibilities to go and anyone who felt they could not go was given the option to stand down.

Corporal John Morgan DAVIES
124th Field Company Royal Engineers
Killed in action 11th July 1916 Mametz Wood
Thiepval Memorial, France

Commemorated at Mametz Wood by great-nephew Meirion Hughes who writes;

My first recollection of knowing of John Morgan's death was when I was taken up to the local cemetery for the first time one Sunday afternoon following chapel. I was a young boy at that time and understood little other than the fact that flowers were being left on a grave in remembrance of someone. Etched into the gravestone was the name of 'Mametz Wood' which, thereafter, was etched into my memory. It was only on later visits that I realized that the grave was *empty*; it was only a focal point of remembrance erected by the family.

John Morgan Davies had no known grave but lies somewhere in a place called Mametz Wood, killed in the Great War. The family would have visited the empty grave in Treorchy cemetery but no one had ever ventured to the old battlefields of France. The photo above shows him in his garden. The young woman is unknown.

My great uncle John Morgan Davies was the son of coal miner Morgan Davies and his wife Elizabeth. He lived with his parents and 3 siblings at 21 Illtyd Street, Treorchy, Rhondda, Glamorganshire. He was a single man and was formerly employed at Dare Colliery, part of the Park and Dare complex (Ocean Coal Co.) in the nearby village of Cwmparc, Rhondda.

He enlisted at the age of 18 in 1914 just after the outbreak of war. He was described as a promising student at the area mining school, so he would have likely joined the Royal Engineers because of his experience working and studying whilst employed at the colliery. His promotion to corporal would also likely reflect his engineering capabilities. I have one of his books that indicates the geological strata of the South Wales Coalfield.

The 124th Field Company Royal Engineers was raised at Porthcawl, a south Wales seaside town, in January 1915, moving to Abergavenny Monmouthshire for training later in the month. The 124th was assigned to the 38th (Welsh) Division in April 1915, embarking for Le Havre, France on 1st December 1915. From January 1916 until June of that year, the division helped to hold the British XI Corps line from Givenchy to Picantin.

On 10th June 1916, the 38th Division received their orders to proceed south in preparation for the Somme offensive and, on 5 July, the division was ordered to prepare for their attack on Mametz Wood, the largest wood on the Somme Battlefield.

On Tuesday 11 July, during one of the Division's attacks on the western side of the Wood, John Morgan Davies was reported as missing in action. Very little is known about what happened to him. An extract from the 124 Field Coy war diary for that day states –

'Mametz Wood. Constructing strong points on the western flank of Wood, at junction of bottom edge of Wood railway, also at junction of Wood Support trench with Wood, also consolidation of near Front Line. Casualties – 2 officers wounded, 3 OR killed 16 OR wounded 5 OR missing.'

Prior to the planned afternoon attack into the northern part of the Wood by the Division on the 11th of July, there was a massive British artillery barrage on those areas of the Wood still held by the Germans. Many shells, however, fell short, causing casualties among the Welsh soldiers awaiting the attack. In reply, the Germans responded to the presumed oncoming attack with their own counter barrage causing many more Welsh casualties. It is, therefore, not known which side's shells were responsible for the death of my great uncle and his comrades on that day.

The name of my great uncle, along with those of Sergeant Horace Frank Anderson and Sapper Henry Cox, is commemorated on Thiepval Memorial, thus being three of the five men stated in the war diary to be 'missing'. The other two soldiers reported as missing must have been found later, as only these three names aforementioned are listed on the Roll of Honour in respect of operations at Mametz Wood on the 11th of July 1916 and commemorated at Thiepval.

The high total number of casualties sustained by the 38th Division during the fateful battle for Mametz Wood is reported as being around 4000 Officers and other ranks, to include 565 dead and 585 'missing' out of a Divisional total of about 18,500 men over the six days of actions. The three Infantry Brigades of 12,000 men had lost a third of their fighting strength. Many still lie in the wood today.

I have a 1916 extract from the local Rhondda newspaper that reads; 'Corporal John Morgan Davies has been reported missing since some weeks'. The number of missing would have included some taken prisoner but, in reality, most would have been found to have been killed and would thereafter remain permanently recorded as 'missing'.

Prior to the centenary of the Somme offensive, I had visited Mametz Wood and the Thiepval Memorial many times but never ventured in detail to the western side of the Wood. Therefore, my pilgrimage on 11th July 2016 had been planned as being the appropriate date to seek out the ground where my great uncle John Morgan died and still lies. On that summer afternoon, I placed a personalised wooden cross of remembrance for John Morgan just inside the Wood at the furthest distance that I had reached, having passed by the sites of the old trench lines referred to in the war diary. It was a perfectly quiet place without any natural or external noise and in order to give a voice to the fallen, I read aloud a part of John McCrae's most poignant poem 'In Flanders Fields' translated into Welsh which was John Morgan's first language and the mother tongue of most of the Welsh who fought and died in Mametz Wood.

I am sure that John Morgan would have felt real comfort at the thought that one hundred years later, someone from his family would be visiting his grave and had duly remembered him for making the final sacrifice.

Editor's note:

The Hampstead Pals have visited Mametz Wood on many occasions, the last being on Sunday 20th October 2019 when a poppy wreath was laid at the 'Dragon Memorial' to the memory of the 38th Welsh Division and our *Welsh Pals* beautifully sang 'Cwm Rhondda' and 'Myfanwy' in their native language. Prior to that, John Grieve spoke about the fight for the wood and the appalling cost in Welsh lives. His quotes, carefully chosen, are appropriate but heartrending;

> 'The watcher at the fire-step began to hope that his friends would so make an end of their work so spread their tea-napery of news-sheets, to make the dixie boil to synchronise with his relief.
> The last direct radiance gave out, his wire and rising glacis, went cold and unillumined, yet clearly defined in an evenly distributed after-visibility. The cratered earth, of all growing things bereaved, bore that uncreaturely impressiveness of telescope-observed bodies - where even pterodactyl would feel the place unfriendly. His mates came from the building-up, and work of restoration the watched dixie almost boiled. Watcyn had already opened the Dairymaid canned butter, it was just light enough to know the green and gilt of the enamelled tin. It was an extremely good brand'.
>
> David Jones. *In Parenthesis.* (London Faber and Faber 1937)

> 'At 4 am on July 15th, we struck the Meaulte-Fricourt-Bazentin road, which ran through 'Happy Valley', and reached the more recent battle area. Wounded and prisoners came streaming past in the half-light. I was shocked by the dead horses and mules; human corpses were all very well but it seemed wrong for animals to be dragged into the war like this. We marched by platoon at fifty yards distance. Just beyond Fricourt, a German shell-barrage made the road impassable; so we left it and moved forward over thickly shell-pitted ground until 8 am, when we found ourselves on the fringe of Mametz Wood, among the dead of our own New Army battalion who had helped capture it. There we halted in thick mist'.
>
> Robert Graves *Goodbye to All That* (London Jonathan Cape 1929)

> 'I want to have a word with you,' he said, drawing me away. 'I've got some bad news for you.' 'What's happened to my young brother . . . is he hit?'

'You know the last message you sent out to try and stop the barrage . . . well, he was one of the runners that took it. He hasn't come back.' ...as dawn was breaking over Bazentin, I turned towards the green shape of Mametz Wood and shuddered in a farewell to one, and to many. I had not even buried him, nor was his grave ever found.

Wyn Griffith *Up to Mametz*. (London. Faber and Faber 1931

The Thiepval Memorial to the Missing

Private John (Jack) DEAN
7th Battalion, The Border Regiment
Missing in Action 23rd April 1917
Arras Memorial, France

Commemorated at The Arras Memorial to the Missing by great-nephew Nick Batt,
Chief Inspector Metropolitan Police (Rtd), who writes;

Thanks to The Hampstead Pals, myself and my two sons, Dominic and Lewis, have
remembered our great-great-uncle Jack Dean many times now, both at the Arras
Memorial to the Missing and where he fell in Happy Valley on 23rd April 1917 at the
Battle of Arras. He was just 20 years and 7 months old and a labourer when he joined
the 7th Battalion The Border Regiment on 24th July 1915 in Blackburn, Lancashire.
Jack was one of three brothers from North Wales who joined up to fight with the
Border Regiment - and he was the one who never came home. He was killed on St

George's Day 1917 - and what happened to his battalion is described dramatically in *Cheerful Sacrifice.*

Unfortunately, the family no longer have any photographs of Jack Dean. We were, however, proud of my son Lewis when he laid a wreath for Jack at the Arras Memorial in 2015. The Pals also took us to Happy Valley Cemetery, a remote and intimate little cemetery that lies on the old Arras battlefield. The lie of the land has changed little although the trenches have gone. The 7th Borders went 'over the top' from a nearby trench and it gave me great joy and pride to toast his memory together with my sons, Dominic and Lewis, with Talisker whisky - his favourite whisky - and now one of mine! It was one of the best-selling single malt whiskies in the country at the turn of the century. When my mother was a young girl in the 1940s, she always remembered Jack's framed photo in the farmhouse kitchen of her great-aunt and a bottle of Talisker next to it on the mantelpiece. I regret that I cannot locate his photograph. However, I can locate a bottle of Talisker!

Well done, Jack.

Editor's note(s):

Taking part in his first attack at zero hour was another youngster, seventeen-year-old Private Reg Eveling. As the only 'southerner' in his company of the 7th Border Regiment, Eveling felt he was regarded as something of a 'foreigner' at first. Fortunately, this did not last.

Just prior to the attack, the Colonel of the Borders had issued this final order; 'Bayonets will be fixed for dealing with the enemy at close quarters with the cold steel'. Unfortunately for this battalion, it would not get anywhere near the enemy on 23 April, having been spotted as it moved to the jumping off trench in Happy Valley, just south of Lone Copse.

Reg Eveling was interviewed on tape by author, Jon Nicholls, in 1985 at his home in Chelmsford, Essex and his dramatic eyewitness account of the destruction of the 7th Border Regiment is shown here in full and was taken from *Cheerful Sacrifice:*

> "The vast majority of these men were either coal miners, dales men or farmers, but all from Kendal, Whitehaven, Cockermouth, Workington and the surrounding villages; as grand a body of men as one could wish to meet and, once I had learned to understand the dialect, I was accepted as one of themselves. Now, this brings me to the day I shall never forget - April 23rd

1917, St George's Day, the day when very few of my pals came back. It was my first and last action. I remember arriving in the trench and it was full of mud. The fire step was broken down so we had to scramble up over the parapet. Well, I was totally terrified but the lads tried to buck me up a bit – but I suppose it felt like you were trying to commit suicide. 'This is the end,' I thought. 'My last day,'… and then came the order; 'Over!' And when you got an order in the army, it had to be *done* and you *did it*. Well, as soon as we went over, I kept well back from the creeping barrage. I was very frightened. You could see the shells bursting only fifty yards in front. Then we came to the barbed wire and it wasn't properly cut… it was sheer murder that was. There were paths cut through the wire and, like animals, we crowded into the paths. That's where most of our casualties came from; machine guns were trained on the gaps and blokes just fell in heaps. Somehow, I got through that OK and kept on going, but then I looked to my left and to my right and couldn't see another soul. To my utter dismay, I was on my own. I panicked and dived into the nearest shell hole and stopped there until it was dark. That was one of the longest days of my life. When I crawled back, a Scots Regiment had taken over our bit of the line and were going to shoot me as they thought I was a German. I never saw a single German that day, yet the whole battalion was wiped out."

The destruction of the 7th Border Regiment, in which Jack Dean was killed, could not be better told. The battalion had lost 15 officers and 404 other ranks out of the 19 officers and 505 men who had gone into action – 204 of them listed as 'Missing'.

The Arras Memorial and Faubourg d'Amiens Cemetery.

The Commonwealth War Graves Commission says;

The French handed over the town of Arras to Commonwealth forces in the spring of 1916 and the system of tunnels upon which the town is built were used and dramatically developed in preparation for the major offensive planned for April 1917.

The Commonwealth section of the FAUBOURG D'AMIENS CEMETERY was begun in March 1916, behind the French military cemetery established earlier. It continued to be used by field ambulances and fighting units until November 1918. The cemetery was enlarged after the Armistice when graves were brought in from the battlefields and from two smaller cemeteries in the vicinity.

The cemetery contains over 2,650 Commonwealth burials of the First World War, 10 of which are unidentified. The graves in the French military cemetery were removed after the war to other burial grounds and the land they had occupied was used for the construction of the Arras Memorial and Arras Flying Services Memorial.

The adjacent ARRAS MEMORIAL commemorates almost 35,000 servicemen from the United Kingdom, South Africa and New Zealand who died in the Arras sector between the spring of 1916 and 7 August 1918, the eve of the Advance to Victory, and who have no known grave. The most conspicuous events of this period were the Arras offensive of April-May 1917 and the German attack in the spring of 1918. Canadian and Australian servicemen killed in these operations are commemorated by memorials at Vimy and Villers-Bretonneux. A separate memorial remembers those killed in the Battle of Cambrai in 1917.

The adjacent ARRAS FLYING SERVICES MEMORIAL (illustrated above) commemorates almost 1,000 airmen of the Royal Naval Air Service, the Royal Flying Corps and the Royal Air Force, either by attachment from other arms of the forces of the Commonwealth or by original enlistment, who were killed on the whole Western Front and who have no known grave.

During the Second World War, Arras was occupied by United Kingdom forces headquarters until the town was evacuated on 23 May 1940. Arras then remained in German hands until it was retaken by Commonwealth and Free French forces on 1 September 1944. The 1939-1945 War burials number 8 and comprise 3 soldiers and 4 airmen from the United Kingdom and 1 entirely unidentified casualty. Located between the 2 special memorials of the 1914-1918 War is the special memorial commemorating an officer of the United States Army Air Force who died during the 1939-1945 War. This special memorial is inscribed with the words "Believed to be buried in this cemetery". In addition, there are 30 war graves of other nationalities, most of them German.

Both cemetery and memorial were designed by Sir Edwin Lutyens, with sculpture by Sir William Reid Dick. The memorial was unveiled by Lord Trenchard, Marshal of the Royal Air Force and Commissioner of the Metropolitan Police on the 31st July 1932 (originally it had been scheduled for 15 May, but due to the sudden death of French President Doumer, as a mark of respect, the ceremony was postponed until July).

The Arras Memorial to the Missing

Captain Gordon Muriel FLOWERDEW VC

Lord Strathcona's Horse (Royal Canadians)
Died of Wounds 31st March 1918
Namps-Au-Val Cemetery

Commemorated at Namps-Au-Val Cemetery by great-niece
Coral Minnifie and her cousin Mary Flowerdew

Coral Minnifie writes;

In May 2013, together with the Hampstead Pals, we visited the grave of our relative, Gordon Flowerdew VC. He was a man who fought for a cause, inspired his comrades and some say turned the tide of the Great War.

Gordon Muriel Flowerdew was born at Billingford Hall, Norfolk on the 2nd of January 1885 to Hannah and Arthur, a gentleman farmer. He was one of 10 sons and 14 children, and, like his brothers, was educated at Framlingham College. His sister Florence described him as being fidgety and full of go, whilst his mother Hannah said he was quiet and reliable and hated fuss or heroics and would have blushed like a girl if anyone said he was a hero.

Shortly after leaving school, he contracted pleurisy and it was considered that a change of climate was urgently needed, so, at the age of 18, he headed for Canada where the family had some connections.

Eventually, he settled in a small agricultural community in Walhachin, British Colombia, an area known as 'Little England' which was a fruit-farming venture aimed at 'gentleman horticulturists.'

He was a storekeeper in 1911 and also a volunteer in the local troop of the 31st British Colombia Horse and became renowned for his excellent horsemanship and for being a marksman. He was also a temporary lawman who achieved celebrity status with the capture of a couple of notorious outlaws who were on the run after robbing a store and brutally beating the proprietor.

War broke out in August 1914, and, of the 45 male settlers listed as living in Walhachin, 44 immediately volunteered to fight and amongst them was Gordon who joined 'B' Squadron Lord Strathcona's Horse. After crossing the Atlantic, 8 months of training was conducted in England as part of the Canadian Cavalry Brigade, known as 'The sore-assed brigade', under the command of Brigadier General J.E.B Seely CB. D.S.O. MP, known as 'Galloper Jack.'

Initially, the cavalry was a stopgap for the infantry in May 1915, with their horses arriving almost a year later. Gordon had a flair for soldiering and rose from Lance Corporal in September 1914 to being commissioned temporary lieutenant in March 1916. Shortly before this, the Strathcona's had resumed their mounted role, and, armed with swords, reacquainted themselves with cavalry drill.

The Strathcona's followed up the German retreat of the Hindenburg Line in spring 1917 and the cavalry also had success at Arras and Cambrai in 1917, however, once again they were required to support the British Line in the role of infantrymen. The Strathcona's also served as the 'trench party' on the front line in early 1918.

On returning from leave in March 1918, Gordon took command of C Squadron, billeted at Ennemain in the department of the Somme. The massive German offensive

'The Kaiser's Battle' had begun on 21st March 1918 and struck a devastating blow against the thinly spread and over-stretched British positions of the Fifth Army.

On the evening of the 29th March 1918, instructions were received to 'Stand by your horses' and be ready to move off at 0530hrs. On the 30th March 1918, Jack Seely informed the French 125th Division Commander that 'We must retake Moreuil Ridge' whose wooded slopes were full of Germans.

The plan was for one squadron to gallop around the North Eastern reaches and for two to press directly into the wood. It was the last real cavalry charge of the Great War and the fighting was fierce with one troop encountering heavy machine-gun fire, dismounting and charging on foot. The squadrons were split. Seely wanted a second attempt to reach the men fighting in the woods.

The task fell to Gordon Flowerdew's Squadron. Dismounted Cavalrymen, led by Lt Fred Harvey VC – an Irish Rugby International - entered the wood and Gordon's Squadron were to meet the Germans as they left the wood. What the Squadron found was a solid line packed with German troops some 300 yards ahead.

Gordon's Mounted Squadron of 75 men armed with swords, charged twice into the murderous fire of 20 machine guns. Gordon was badly wounded with two bullets in the chest and grievous wounds to his thighs. He died the following day on 31st March in No 41 Casualty Clearing Station southwest of Amiens. Gordon lived long enough to be made aware of the success of the charge

The Strathcona's diarist said, 'The charge led by Gordon had a great moral effect on those still fighting in the wood. Thinking themselves surrounded, their resistance to the dismounted troops weakened considerably.' Jack Seely wrote, 'His splendid courage and fearless leading turned the fortunes of that fateful day' He further stated that his final act had been 'not only one of the bravest, but also one of the most decisive of the war.'

Jack Seely also wrote to Gordon's sister, referring to 'when your brave young brother met his death at the moment of victory to which he had contributed the largest share.' A posthumous Victoria Cross was announced a few weeks later, recognising his 'great valour,' the citation for which read;

For most conspicuous bravery and dash when in command of a squadron detailed for special services of a very important nature. On reaching his first objective, Lieutenant Flowerdew saw two lines of enemy, each about sixty strong, with machine guns in the centre and flanks; one line being about two hundred yards behind the other. Realizing the critical nature of the operation and how much depended on it, Lieut. Flowerdew ordered a troop under Lieut. Harvey, VC, to dismount and carry out a special movement, while he led the remaining three troops to the charge. The squadron (less one troop) passed over both lines, killing many of the enemy with the sword, and wheeling about galloping on them again. Although the squadron had then lost about 70 per cent of its members, killed and wounded from rifle and machine-gun fire directed on it from the front and both flanks, the enemy broke and retired. The survivors of the squadron then established themselves in a position where they were joined, after much hand-to-hand fighting, by Lieut. Harvey's party. Lieut. Flowerdew was dangerously wounded through both thighs during the operation but continued to cheer his men. There can be no doubt that this officer's great valour was the prime factor in the capture of the position.

Charge of Flowerdew's Squadron, 1918 by Alfred Munnings, Canadian War Museum

Editor's Note:

The Hampstead Pals have visited Moreuil Wood, the site of the VC action and Gordon Flowerdew's grave, on two occasions, in 2013 and 2018. The Cemetery is a little off the 'usual' battlefield route and is not near the scene of Gordon Flowerdew's VC action in which he lost his life.

The village of Namps-au-Val lies about 16 kilometres southwest of Amiens. It was made as a result of the 'Kaiser's Battle' the great 21 March 1918 German Offensive which pushed back the British 5th Army almost to Amiens. Casualty Clearing Stations were set up by the 41st, 50th and 55th Divisions and they remained there until the middle of April. Almost all the burials in the cemetery were carried out by them but nine graves in Plot II, Row D, were brought after the Armistice from Conty French Military Cemetery. The cemetery contains 408 Commonwealth burials of the First World War and an Army Service Corps driver, Harold Jocelyn aged 21, from the Dunkirk Retreat in May 1940. There are also 16 French war graves. The cemetery was designed by Sir Reginald Blomfield.

Captain David Philip HIRSCH VC
4th Battalion, The Yorkshire Regiment
Killed in action at the Battle of Arras 23rd April 1917

Commemorated at Kestrel Copse, Guemappe & The Arras Memorial France by niece
Pamela Holliday & grand-nephew Jarvis Browning, who writes;

This all started in 2012 through a chance meeting with a battlefield guide who put us
in touch with Jon Nicholls (Via The Hampstead Pals website), the author of the
definitive book on the Battle of Arras, 'Cheerful Sacrifice.' He took myself and my aunt,
Pamela Holliday, to France on 23 April 2012.

It was 95 years after his death in action and we wanted to locate the scene of Uncle
Phil's last stand during the bloody Battle of Arras in which he won the Victoria Cross.
I had made a Celtic Cross, a replica of the original that the Green Howards had placed
near to where he was killed, at a lonely place called Kestrel Copse, near the little village

of Geumappe. His grave was never found as the ground had soon been retaken by the enemy. Consequently, his name is now on the Arras Memorial to the Missing.

We set off from Arras and retraced the steps the battalion would have taken from the Arras chalk caves (which we visited the day before) and followed their route to Kestrel Copse, a little wood, so named by the British soldiers and the scene of their fateful attack that day and where they came under intense rifle and machine-gun fire from the enemy lines from three directions, making the position impossible to hold.

Captain Philip Hirsch was rallying his men to make a good job of defence in an almost impossible situation. He was on his feet and hence a prime target to the enemy. having been wounded already. When you go there and see where the actual VC exploit occurred, you can see that it was an utterly hopeless task. If you follow the trench line from the corner of the wood to the brow behind, you get a better picture of the lay of the land and how exposed to fire the 4th Yorkshires were. It made the hair stand up on the back of my neck. We placed the replica cross at the corner of the wood, at the edge of an old trench line near the Cherisy road, said a few words and prayers and departed. It is an exposed place and the wind was bitterly cold. The next time we visited the wood it was five years later, on the occasion of the 100th anniversary of Uncle Phil's death. A wonderful ceremony was organised by the Mayor, Monsieur Reynald Roche and the good people of Geumappe who have taken it upon themselves to 'keep watch' over Uncle Phil and have adopted him as their own hero. Many of our family members attended, some from South Africa, and the whole weekend, transport, accommodation at the Moderne Hotel and battlefield tour, plus a special ceremony at the Arras Memorial was organised by Jon and Rick Jackson (our driver) of the Hampstead Pals.

The ceremony, on the weekend of the 100ᵗʰ Anniversary of Phillip Hirsch's death, was attended by members of the Hirsch family; Jarvis Browning (centre photo in bowler hat), Mrs Pamela Holliday (Nee Hirsch) to the right of Jarvis (wearing beret) and Phillip Kilpin (great-nephew) to the right of photo holding wreath. Also in the picture wearing medals is Lt Colonel Anthony Gaynor MBE The Green Howards

Great-nephew Phillip Kilpin writes;

David Philip Hirsch, known as 'Pip', was born on 28th December 1896 to Harry and Edith Hirsch of Weetwood Grove, Leeds. In December 1914, Pip had come, almost directly, from Willaston School, Nantwich, where he was head boy and an outstanding athlete, to the army, where he was commissioned in April 1915. He was barely 18 years old and it was certainly a case of 'Schoolboy into War.'

Photo: Phillip Kilpin

A sunny day in the trenches of the Somme. Lt Phillip Hirsch in shirtsleeves

He arrived in France in early 1916 where he was attached to the 4th Yorkshire Regiment and served with them at High Wood and the capture of Eaucourt l'Abbaye during the Battle of the Somme. He had been wounded in September 1916 and mentioned in dispatches. He was also promoted to Lieutenant and, in March 1917, to Captain. His heroic action of 23 April 1917 (which has been well documented elsewhere) resulted in the VC being gazetted in June 1917 and presented by King George V to his parents at Buckingham Palace.

For most conspicuous bravery and devotion to duty in attack. Having arrived at the first objective, Capt. Hirsch, although already twice wounded, returned over fire-swept slopes to satisfy himself that the defensive flank was being established. Machine-gun fire was so intense that it was necessary for him to be continuously up and down the line encouraging his men to dig and hold the position. He continued to encourage his men by standing on the parapet and steadying them in the face of machine-gun fire and counter-attack until he was killed. His conduct throughout was a magnificent example of the greatest devotion to duty.

On the morning of Saturday 22nd April 2017 (due to the French Elections of the 23rd), we all got together to commemorate Capt. David Philip Hirsch's death near Kestrel Copse. It was early in the morning and bitterly cold, a nasty wind blowing and the odd light rain squall. I imagined the conditions were similar to the morning that Philip died. It felt as if he was with us... Amazingly, the people of Guemappe had erected a headstone to Philip with a picture of him embedded in it. They had also taken the wooden cross left there by Pam and Jarvis in 2012 and sealed it in transparent plastic and erected it there too. They organised a section of 12 standard-bearers for the occasion. These included 2 of our young family members and David Wardel of the Green Howards. The Memorial was unveiled by Pamela Holliday and the Mayor, Monsieur Roche. Colonel Anthony Gaynor MBE of the Green Howards spoke, as did the Mayor. Great-nieces Hazel Docherty and Sarah Barrett replied, speaking in French. The whole contingent then attended a mayoral reception at the Guemappe Town Hall afterwards. The kindness and generosity of our French hosts were amazing. On the morning of the 23rd, we all visited the Arras Memorial where we held a private service. Sarah Barret read the VC Citation. Colonel Anthony Gaynor gave a short account of what actually happened on that fateful day, 100 years ago. The ceremony was also attended by Mr Nigel Stevens of the Commonwealth War Graves Commission. I found the whole experience heart-wrenching and it still brings tears to my eyes. Wasn't it just incredible that Pip had time, during the heat of battle, to make notes? What were his thoughts when he realised that he was the last officer standing and that there was no hope of survival? I realise now, after reading the letters to his parents and family, that we have missed getting to know a man who would have developed into somebody very special. Our whole family is the poorer for not having had the chance to know him but also richer in the knowledge of what he sacrificed for all of us.

Photo: Fabrice Thery

Kestrel Copse 2017

Editor's Note:

The war diary of the 4th Yorks records that the attack on the 23 April had gone in at 4.40 am and by 8.10 am, the remnants of the battalion were back in their own front line, the attack having failed. No unwounded prisoners were taken and casualties were 3 officers killed, 7 wounded and 1 missing, believed killed. 352 other ranks were killed, wounded or missing; the proportions not immediately ascertained. It is now known that at least 109 men of the 4th Yorks Battalion were killed in action on the 23rd.

86 have no known grave and are commemorated on the Arras Memorial together with the name of 'Uncle Phil' Hirsch VC, whose last scribbled field notes (now in the possession of Phillip Kilpin) recorded;

"It looks like I am the only officer of the Yorks still standing. I am ready for heaven."

Private George Stanley MILLER
1/5th Norfolk Regiment
Killed in action 12th August 1915
Helles Memorial, Gallipoli

Commemorated at Azmak Cemetery & The Helles Memorial Gallipoli by great-nephew Clive Harris, Ex-Royal Signals & Hertfordshire Constabulary, who writes;

As a small boy, two things stick in my mind when visiting my great-grandmother. First, her broad Norfolk accent, a rural twang unheard in my London-bred family; secondly, a pair of brass shell cases above her fireplace recording a soldier 'who fell at Suvla Bay…' Where was this place? *'That was your great-grandad's brother; he disappeared into a strange-shaped cloud never to be seen again'.*

By the time I was a teenager, the Great War played a far larger part in my life. Through the veterans I met on my paper round and the local Western Front Association meetings, I became obsessed with the First World War, which was, by this time, a fast-fading memory that had taken place some 65 years earlier. Like many, my focus was the Somme & Ypres with increasingly numerous weekend trips to the 'old front line'. Then, when my 95-year-old great-grandmother died, I inherited a box full of 'old stuff' among which were the memories of my uncle George.

George Stanley Miller had had a tough start in life. Born in 1886, he was raised in the notorious Row Housing area of Great Yarmouth. In 1911, his address is given as No14, Row 36. A 'Sawmill Machinist', he still lived at home along with his four siblings, among them my great-grandfather Charlie Miller. Charlie was to move to London with his wife after the Great War to start a new life as a milkman, then he, alongside George and a third brother Ernie, joined the local Territorial battalion, the 1/5 Norfolk's.

As part of the 54th (East Anglian) Division, they initially patrolled the coastline before mobilising to Hertfordshire for overseas training in and around St Albans. In late July 1915, the brothers embarked for the Dardanelles on the RMS Aquitania and landed at Suvla Bay on 10th August, just four days after the initial landings. The whole battlefront at Suvla was in a state of flux, so to push forward the line to join Kiretch Tepe to Chocolate Hill, a hasty, ill-prepared advance was ordered for mid-afternoon on the 12th. Along with the 1/5th Suffolk's and 1/8th Hampshire's (Isle of Wight Rifles), the 163rd Brigade advanced, but without artillery support and with no opportunity for reconnaissance, it soon broke down. The Norfolk's, led by their commanding officer Sir Horace Proctor Beauchamp, cane in hand, found themselves making progress ahead of the flanking battalions. Advancing amid a hornet's nest of Turkish sniper posts and defensive positions, they were soon cut off and alone. Firing continued until early evening when the battlefield fell silent. Over the next few days, numerous wounded made their way back to the British front line, however, the scene of the battalion's last stand was never reached and when Suvla was evacuated in late December, 138 men remained missing, among them George Stanley Miller.

Due to the number of Sandringham estate workers in the battalion, the King took a personal interest in their fate, Sir Ian Hamilton's official Gallipoli Despatches did little to provide the answer:

'But the Colonel, with sixteen officers and 250 men, still kept pushing on, driving the enemy before them. Nothing more was ever seen or heard of any

of them. They charged into the forest and were lost to sight or sound. Not one of them ever came back.'

It was after the war that the mystery was finally solved; during the establishment of cemeteries by the Imperial War Graves Commission, the Reverend Pierrepoint Edwards MC (who had been the brigade padre during the campaign) wrote in 1919:

We have found the 5th Norfolk's... They were scattered over an area of about one square mile, at a distance of at least 800 yards behind the Turkish front line. Many of them had evidently been killed on a farm, as a local Turk, who owns the place, told us that when he came back, he found the farm covered with the decomposing bodies of British soldiers, which he threw into a small ravine. The whole thing quite bears out the original theory that they did not go very far on, but got mopped up one by one, all except the ones who got into the farm'.

Today, George lies, with his comrades, in an unmarked plot of the beautiful Azmak Cemetery and his name is recorded on the stunning Helles Memorial that looks out over the Aegean Sea. I have visited him several times a year over the last three decades, with members of the *Hampstead Pals* joining me in 2012. If I could have only one day to visit the battlefields, it would be to Gallipoli I would go as I still have far more questions than answers after 30 years of research.

George Stanley Miller is in our memory far more today than when I first glimpsed those brass shell cases that I still treasure. Our knowledge of his service life and death is far greater than it was for those that knew and mourned him and his legacy lives on through my son, now 15, 'George' Addam Harris.

He will never be forgotten.

Editor's Note:

In May 2012, The Hampstead Pals made a memorable visit to Gallipoli under the excellent organisation and leadership of Clive Harris.

Clive has also been an assistant guide on several Hampstead Pals Tours.

Gallipoli. Clive Harris (L) with Colin Butler MBE

Corporal Alexander Everett ROSS

49th Battalion (Edmonton Regiment) Canadian
Expeditionary Force
Died of wounds received in action 15 August 1918
Villers-Bretonneux Military Cemetery

Found & commemorated at Villers-Bretonneux Military Cemetery by family friends
John and Gilli Grieve on behalf of Patti Homer

Bruce Coleman (Royal Canadian Mounted Police) writes;

This is the story of just one Canadian soldier. It is written on behalf of our good friend
and neighbour Patti Homer who asked the Hampstead Pals to visit her great-uncle's
grave in France on their next visit. This was duly carried out on 24 May 2018.

It is a story of recognition and remembrance and begins in Sooke, British Columbia where descendants of Alex Ross currently live. Patti is the great-niece of Alex Ross and was aware that we had travelled to France to visit the WW1 battlegrounds with the Hampstead Pals.

Patti learned from her mother of the demise of her great-uncle, Alexander Ross, on the battlefields of France. Alex was born in Shawville, Quebec, on 16 February 1896. He was one of nine children, eight girls and one boy. In civvy street, he was a schoolteacher and single man. On 3 March 1916, at the age of 20, he had enlisted 'for the duration' in Edmonton, Alberta and had sailed for France on the SS 'Olympia' on 14 November 1916 arriving in England on 21 November. He was posted to France on 29 December 1916. He was to be badly wounded twice, the second time fatally on 15 August 1918, near Parvillers, France.

The family had lost the details of Alex's death in action and the actual location of his grave. This vital information about his death and final resting place had remained a mystery for over 100 years. It is hard to conceive the questions, sadness and grief brought upon the Ross family by not knowing what had become of their beloved brother so close to Armistice Day, 11 November 1918.

In 2017, we had hosted a dinner at our home in Sooke and Patti Homer had joined us, meeting our guests, John and Gilli Grieve. Over the course of dinner, the subject came up about Alexander Ross and the mystery of his demise. This was the beginning of the end of Alex's story, which was to spark an interesting investigation, by studying his service file and the 49th Battalion war diary, to finally determine how and where this young man had died.

Patti submitted a request to the Canadian Archives, Ottawa, Canada, in June 2017 and discovered the Archives were in the process of digitizing all the WW1 records for the general public. After a short wait, she was to receive Alex's service file in its entirety and it was through reading this that she discovered that Alex had been killed in action and later buried at Villers-Bretonneux, France.

A brief summary of his service file and a study of the war diary reveals that Alexander Ross joined the Canadian Expeditionary Force on 3 March 1916. He was then transferred to the UK and then France later that year. On 8 June 1917, he was wounded in a massive trench raid by the 7th Canadian Brigade at Avion just north of Vimy Ridge. The Canadians had gained a fearsome reputation for trench raiding and this large raid was no exception.

Alex had certainly been in the thick of the action, whereby he received gunshot wounds to his left arm, left thigh and left calf muscle. 'Gunshot' wounds could also mean wounds from shrapnel, shell or bomb fragments. He was initially sent to Étaples and then to the UK for treatment. He reached Birmingham on 23 June 1917 and was treated in The No 1 Southern General Hospital at Dudley Road. He recuperated there for several weeks and was finally discharged on 31 August 1917 but remained at Bramshott Camp, Hants until 22 November before returning to the front, fortunately missing the bloody battle of Passchendaele in which his battalion had been heavily involved.

On 22 June 1918, Alex was promoted to Lance Corporal. On 20 July, he was granted 'Special Leave' to Paris. We can only speculate that Alex may have, most probably, indulged in the odd croissant, maybe a couple of beers and a few glasses of vin rouge!

It was during the savage fighting at Blucher Wood near Parvillers, on 13 August 1918 (and ironically, on the day he had been promoted to full corporal), that Alex had been badly wounded by gunshot to the lower back and right wrist. He was transferred to No 48 Casualty Clearing Station at Dury Asylum Hospital in Amiens, but sadly, died there on 15 August. He was buried in the nearby Dury Hospital Cemetery. In September 1927, his remains were exhumed by the Imperial War Graves Commission and taken to the newly constructed cemetery at Villers-Bretonneux for re-burial.

On 24 May 2018, with thanks to the Hampstead Pals, a simple memorial service was held at the grave of Alexander Ross at Villers-Bretonneux, whereby his life and army service were celebrated. His memory was also toasted with fine malt whisky in the true spirit of the Hampstead Pals.

I can assure all those people who attended Villers that day that the kind words spoken to commemorate an ordinary Canadian boy were of great comfort for those at home in Sooke, British Columbia.

Lastly, Patti Homer wrote the following:

'I am forever grateful to everyone who has helped my family and me on this incredible journey to find and honour our uncle, Alexander Everett ROSS.

Editor's note *(from original Hampstead Pals Tour Notes made in 1993)*:

The Hampstead Pals have visited Villers-Bretonneux Cemetery and the Australian National War Memorial on many occasions and have always been impressed with the majestic splendour of the dramatic sentinel-like memorial and the cemetery, which contains many Canadian burials from the fierce fighting of 1918. It is a real 'Commonwealth Cemetery' in the true sense.

The small town of Villers-Bretonneux, which lies only 16 kilometres east of Amiens, was the key to the defence of that important city and the Germans, in their great advance of March 1918, were set on taking it. From here, you can get an excellent view of the battlefield, west to the city of Amiens and north to the Somme where you can see the Thiepval Memorial from the Memorial tower on a clear day.

On April 4th, after a heavy bombardment, fifteen German divisions launched a ferocious attack. The northern thrust was stopped by the British 1st Cavalry and 33rd Battalion AIF. On 17-18 April, in their second attempt to take Villers-Bretonneux, the Germans drenched the woods and valleys behind the town here with mustard gas, causing over 1000 Australian casualties. At dawn on 24 April, the Germans attacked behind tanks and the town was captured.

The Australians launched a massive counter-attack on Anzac Day (25 April) and the town was re-captured after bitter street close-quarter fighting. Brigadier Grogan VC called it the greatest individual feat of the war. On the 2nd of May, Lt Colonel Ray Leane led the 48th Battalion to capture Monument Wood, although 12 officers and 124 men fell casualty.

In this cemetery, there are 2,141 Great War graves including 779 Australians, 267 Canadians and 607 'unknowns.' This is a magnificent concentration cemetery made after the war and the graves come from a wide area. Twenty plots were made in 1920 with eleven plots being entirely Australian graves. Then space had to be found for more graves and a further four plots were added and so it expanded to be the largest cemetery on the 1918 battlefield.

One notable Canadian grave is that of Lt. John Brilliant VC, MC of the 22nd (Quebec) Battalion 'Van Doos', killed while attacking German machine-gun posts on 8 August 1918. He was a French Canadian and the family inscription on his grave is in French and tells how 'he died gloriously in the land of his forefathers' and ends with the words, 'Good blood cannot die' (Plot 6a row B to the left of the Cross of Sacrifice).

There are two Second World War graves at the front of the next plot, plot 7, where two New Zealand crew members of a Mosquito of 487 Squadron RAF are buried. They crashed in April 1945 while taking off from the airfield at Rosières-en-Santerre.

The Australian Memorial commemorates 10,797 named Australians who have no known grave. (A further 5000 are listed on the Menin Gate, Ypres and 1298 at VC Corner, Fromelles.)

The memorial was unveiled by King George V1 in July 1938. A parade takes place on the lawn every Anzac Day. By coincidence, as mentioned, this is the anniversary of the night the Australians took part in the successful counter-attack at Villers-Bretonneux in 1918. Much of the action took place a few hundred yards behind the memorial. Visitors to the memorial will notice the evidence of a firefight and action here in June 1940 when a section of French Senegalese troops placed a machine gun and an observation post at the top of the tower, probably thinking, mistakenly, that the Germans would respect the memorial and not shoot back. One of two German tanks attacking from the direction of Villers-Bretonneux crashed through the southern boundary of the cemetery, then crossed and flattened the headstones of the last two plots of graves on the right (plots 19 & 20) and opened fire on the men at the top of the memorial. A Messerschmitt 109 also machine-gunned the position. The worst of the damage was repaired after the war but bullet marks on the Cross of Sacrifice, the stone gardener's sheds and on some of the headstones were left as honourable scars of war.

Also commemorated on the panels is the name of Private John Pope, born in Mile End, London and the younger brother of Charles Pope VC. He emigrated before his brother to Australia in 1914 and probably encouraged him to come too. He came out to France in 1916, serving with the 51st Battalion AIF and was killed on 25 April 1918 in the counter-attack on Villers-Bretonneux.

Look for the name of Private Eric Pinches DCM, 5th Company Machine Gun Corps on the memorial. He won a DCM at Lagnicourt when he rushed an enemy machine-gun post with bombs and captured the crew. He died on 3 May 1917 from wounds received the previous day at Bullecourt. He came from Ithaca, Brisbane and was only 16 years old; the youngest Australian to die on the Western Front.

The town of Villers-Bretonneux is twinned with Robinvale, Victoria. The town was named after Robin Cuttle, an air-gunner whose plane was shot down at Caix, south of Villers-Bretonneux on 9th May 1918. The township was new and his mother placed a sign up at the new station, 'Welcome to Robinvale' (from the Latin 'farewell Robin'). The name stuck and was adopted. The town houses an impressive Anzac Museum in the school.

Australian National Memorial, Villers–Bretonneux.

From the top of the tower, the view is quite spectacular over the rolling countryside of the Somme, towards Amiens and its cathedral. It is interesting to note that the sprightly veteran soldier, Alf Razzell - at the age of 90 - climbed to the top of the tower after stopping to regain his breath only twice. (I was unkindly accused of attempted murder!) On a circular plaque in the turret are bronze arrows indicating other Australian battlefields on the Western Front and far-away Canberra, Australia's capital city.

This was the last of the great British Empire and Commonwealth World War I memorials to be built in France and Belgium. Just one year later, the Second Great War would happen. Beside the King was his wife, Elizabeth Bowes–Lyon, whose brother, Captain Fergus Bowes–Lyon was killed at the Battle of Loos in France in 1915. Also present were Albert Lebrun, President of France, and Earl Page, Deputy Prime Minister of Australia. To the great crowd assembled on the grassed area in front of the memorial, the King - whose words were being broadcast directly to Australia - spoke of the Australian soldiers, airmen and nurses commemorated at Villers-Bretonneux:

The King's speech reinforced the view that many Australians had formed from their nation's involvement in the 'Great War' and of the heavy price paid in suffering and sacrifice on the battlefields of the Western Front and Gallipoli. That bloodletting had - emphasised the King - allowed the new *Commonwealth* to pass from 'youth to manhood' and to take its 'rightful place in the community of Nations'. From where he spoke, the King sadly observed the long rows of graves in the cemetery, between which all who come to the memorial have to pass, and thus finished his speech with these memorable words:

'They rest in peace, while over them all, Australia's tower keeps watch and ward.'

121

Private Arthur William SEARLE

1st Battalion, The Suffolk Regiment
Killed in action 3rd October 1915
Loos Memorial, France

Found & commemorated at the Loos Memorial by niece Anne Copley who writes:

Arthur William Searle was born on 20th October 1893 in Whittlesey, Cambridgeshire, to William (a farm labourer) and Jane Searle née Asplin. Arthur had 4 siblings, including Lucy Ada Rycroft Searle, my grandmother. He appears in the 1901 census, aged 7, and again in the 1911 census, aged 17, as an agricultural labourer. He never married.

It is likely that he enlisted at the end of January 1915 (and was therefore a 'New Army' recruit). There is a photograph of soldiers enlisting in Whittlesey but he cannot be identified. A letter to his sister gives the information as 'No 1 Platoon, M Company, 3rd Suffolk Regiment (training), Felixstowe'. He then went to France in about June 1915 after a mere five-month training, joining the 1st Suffolk's, a regular army battalion, which was in Khartoum when war was declared and did not arrive in France until mid-January 1915. In April-May, they were heavily involved in the 2nd Battle of Ypres and drafts were urgently needed to bring the battalion up to strength.

During his brief service, he communicated regularly with his sister, Lucy, both by letter and Field Service Postcard from 16 April 1915 to 27 Sept 1915. They are mostly positive but he was finding conditions in the trenches uncomfortable.

The battalion was sent to the Loos sector, reaching Sailly-Labourse on the 28th of September. Four days later, they were moved into support trenches opposite the 'Little Willy' trench at the Hohenzollern Redoubt, which the battalion was ordered to attack on 2-3 October.

The attack was a failure but the close fighting was intense. According to the war diary, the battalion sustained about 160 casualties in this brief visit to the front line. Of these, 32 were killed and most are commemorated on the Loos memorial. Arthur was reported 'missing' on October 3rd. Arthur also appears on the Whittlesey War Memorial. 'The Soldiers Died in the Great War' publication suggests that he died of wounds. Therefore, he was probably picked up by stretcher-bearers and treated at a regimental aid post before succumbing to his wounds.

Had he died from his wounds, there would have been a burial plot but that could have been lost subsequently. The battlefield was not cleared for several years so his body could perhaps not be identified.

In 'The Suffolk and Essex Free Press' of November 3rd, Arthur is listed under 'wounded and missing'. Certainly, his family apparently had correspondence suggesting that he had been seen alive by a comrade, but this was not verified. There is a letter from the War Office saying that there was no further official information on Arthur's whereabouts.

My grandmother, Lucy, never forgot her older brother. She named her only son after him and had a locket containing his photograph. As a child, I remember her talking about him frequently. On a recent visit to Whittlesey to view the War Memorial, a visit to the local museum produced the good fortune of their having his 'Dead Man's Penny' as well as a photograph. It was unclear how they got there.

Editor's note *(based on original Hampstead Pals Tour Notes made in 1993):*

From the A26 Motorway, while speeding to their holiday destinations, thousands of British tourists will see on the left-hand side, looming out of the early morning mist, one of the familiar features of the 1915 Loos battlefield. This is the Double Crassier – huge twin spoil heaps - which dominate this flat mining area for miles around. 'Just another French coalmine' (if there is a comment at all). Very few will know that these mountainous heaps shadow one of the most tragic battlefields of the First World War.

The small town of Loos-en-Gohelle, which lies close to these giant spoil heaps, can be found just to the north of the large town of Lens and is easily reached from the channel ports by following the A26 motorway and exiting at junction 6.1. The A21 can then be followed to Loos. This battlefield can be 'done in a day'. It was in September 1915 that the British Army launched its largest offensive to date on the Western Front - here at Loos.

This was an offensive on a grander scale than the previous battles of Neuve Chapelle and Festubert in terms of artillery, infantry and the frontage attacked. Loos also marked the first use by the British of poison gas, following on from its first use by the Germans at the Second Battle of Ypres some five months earlier.

Unlike Passchendaele and the Somme, the Battle of Loos has received relatively little attention, but an excellent and detailed account of the battle can be found in 'Most Unfavourable Ground' by Niall Cherry. Published in 2005, this is a thorough account of not only what happened on each day of the battle, but also of the events which led up to it and the aftermath (most famously, perhaps, the replacement of Sir John French by Sir Douglas Haig as the British Commander-in-Chief just three months after the battle).

124

Further Editor's note:

Peter Searle is commemorated on the Loos Memorial which encloses the aptly named Dud Corner Cemetery. The name is supposed to have originated from the large number of dud shells that lay around. Driving along the road, and from near the cemetery, the very flat nature of the landscape here can be appreciated. The double crassier is clearly visible. The front of the cemetery is open to the very busy main road, with a stone tower structure at either side

At the left-hand entrance building, steps lead up to a viewing platform which gives excellent views not only of the cemetery itself but also the battlefield beyond. There was a German strongpoint here which was taken by the 15th Division on the first day of the battle. The cemetery walls along the sides and at the back are lined with panels which list the names of the missing.

The Hampstead Pals have visited this beautiful memorial and cemetery many times. After the Armistice, nearly 2,000 graves were concentrated here from the battlefields around, and more than 50% of these are unidentified. This is truly a cemetery reflecting the battle; most of those buried here died during the Battle of Loos and a number of regimental battlefield memorials were brought to the cemetery after the War, including those of the 10th Scottish Rifles and the 17th London Regiment, dating from the Battle of Loos.

The Memorial to the Missing, as stated above, is made up of the 139 panels lining the cemetery on three sides. These commemorate 20,597 men who died in this area (strictly from the River Lys to the old southern boundary of the First Army, east and west of Grenay) and who have no known grave. This will, of course, include many of those who fell at the Battle of Loos. The panels at the back of the cemetery are set in semi-circular and circular alcoves. There are excellent views across the battlefield from the back of the cemetery by the Cross of Sacrifice.

John Kipling.

Rudyard Kipling's son, John, died during the battle of Loos, and for a long time, had 'no known grave'. However, a headstone at St. Mary's ADS Cemetery now bears his name although there is still considerable doubt as to whether or not it is him. On the 100th anniversary of his death, the Hampstead Pals held a 'Court of Enquiry' led by John Grieve at the 'presumed' grave of young Kipling.

An extraordinary new theory arose, that he lies nearby in an unknown officer's grave; an interesting story and worthy of more debate. The story originated from an employee of the CWGC and is derived from a mysterious note *allegedly* found in Kipling's office litter bin a day after his death referring to a grave in St Mary's ADS Cemetery; 'Second grave beneath the tree 'tis you, my son, I know 'tis thee'. (It is interesting to note that the Commonwealth War Graves Commission confirmed two lines of poplar trees in the cemetery were removed in the 60s). Two unknown officers are buried side by side. In the pocket of one was supposedly found a pair of broken spectacles. If so, what happened to them? Surely, Dad would have been made aware of this?

His name still appears here at the Loos Memorial as one of the missing among the Irish Guards on Panel 9. It gives one the uncomfortable impression that the Commonwealth War Graves Commission are still 'unsure.' The only sure way to establish whether John Kipling lies under that headstone would be to sample DNA from the remains, but then the floodgates of demand for similar exhumations would open. The CWGC have, rightly so, confirmed that remains will not be exhumed for DNA to be taken. The debate goes on.

The Dud Corner, Loos Memorial to the Missing and Cemetery
Winter 2013

Serjeant George Robert SCHOFIELD

2nd Battalion, Royal Ulster Rifles
Killed in action 1st November 1944 at the Battle of Overloon.
Venray War Cemetery, Holland

Commemorated at Venray War Cemetery, Holland, by son, Raymond Schofield-Almond who writes;

It was perhaps my fifteenth visit to the small but beautifully maintained Commonwealth War Graves Commission cemetery down a narrow leafy lane on the outskirts of Venray in Holland. The small wooden crosses of remembrance on my dad's grave stood out in bold outline; to see it also covered in fresh flowers came as a great shock. Who had put them there?

My passion for visiting European battlefields had started in 1980 when I took my step-father, Edward John Almond, to visit St Valery-en-Caux for the 40th anniversary of his capture by Rommel. I have continued this passion for visiting the battlefields by travelling with the War Research Society and the Hampstead Pals.

Visiting my real father, Serjeant George Robert Schofield, Royal Ulster Rifles, killed on the night of 31st October-1st November 1944, has become an annual pilgrimage since first discovering where his body had been laid to rest.

On that fateful day in 1944, my mum had been left a young widow with a baby whose father had never seen him. Earlier in 1944, George, like many soldiers, had been assigned to be part of the Normandy invasion. After D-Day, the Royal Ulster Rifles had continued to fight their way into Europe until they reached Holland. There, at the Battle of Overloon, Dad had been killed. He never saw or held me...

After the war, my mother remarried and my surname was changed to Almond. My step-father, Ted Almond, a professional soldier in the East Surreys, after being captured at St Valery-en-Caux in June 1940, had been imprisoned in Stalag 8B/344, Lamsdorf, Germany for five years. He stayed in the army after the war, transferring to the Special Investigation Branch of the Royal Military Police. He was posted around the world with Mum and me, his adopted son, to whom he was a most loving father.

When I was 19, I followed my step-father into the army, joining the Royal Corps of Signals where I qualified as a signaller, travelling to different scenes of conflict, rising to the rank of WO2 until I was injured in a parachuting accident. My specialised knowledge of communications that I had learned in the Army led me into the diplomatic service, before settling down in the city of London as a director of a Japanese merchant bank.

My step-father had often encouraged me to visit my real dad's grave in Holland. After Ted's death, I felt at last able to do that. Then came the chance meeting with the young Dutch couple whereby I learned where dad's grave was to be found.

So, in early 1989, I set off with my wife Jane and son Robert and drove to Holland to visit my father at Venray Cemetery. On entering the cemetery for the first time, I was struck by the peace and tranquillity and was impressed by how beautifully it was maintained. Forty-five years after Dad died, I stood with my family for the first time in front of the white headstone with its simple inscription:

Sjt 7011515 George Robert Schofield, Royal Ulster Rifles, 1st November 1944

Now that I had found Dad, I made up my mind to visit his grave regularly. I also contacted dad's Regimental Association, and, through them, got in touch with some of the men who had fought alongside him. I learnt that Dad had been a highly respected soldier. I even managed to find my dad's best friend, Des, who had been with him when he was shot on return from that fatal night patrol.

In my frequent visits to Venray, the only wreaths that I had ever seen on the grave were the ones I had placed there myself. So, to walk into Venray cemetery one day in September 1998 and see it covered with fresh flowers came as a great surprise. I tried to read the messages on the cards that accompanied the flowers but to no avail as it had been raining and the writing was unreadable. However, a few initials and a possible name could be made out. A quick check in the Commonwealth War Graves Commission visitor's book revealed similar handwriting, and the name of a 'Mrs M' of Laleham, Surrey. I wondered if this could be a friend of my dad? I was led to believe that Dad was an only child.

On my return home, I made some enquiries and managed to identify who it might be. It took me three days to pluck up the courage to ring the number. An older lady answered and I asked if she had recently visited Holland. 'Yes,' came the reply. 'Did you visit Venray Cemetery?' I asked. 'Yes, dear,' came the reply, in a rather inquisitive way. 'Why were you visiting my dad's grave?' I asked. After a moment of silence, the lady said, 'Please tell me it's Raymond I'm speaking to?' I said, 'That's right.' 'Ray Schofield?' she said. 'No, Ray Almond - I was adopted. Who are you?' 'I'm your Auntie Madge,' she said. 'We've been looking for you for over 50 years! I'm your dad's eldest sister!'

Madge and her sister, Joan, had been visiting George's grave every September since 1952. On their most recent visit, they were a week later than usual, otherwise, I might never have seen their flowers and this whole story would have been different. The entire Schofield family welcomed me warmly and Madge, as the oldest surviving family member, arranged a party for everyone else to meet me. The family then decided they would all make a pilgrimage to Venray to visit George's grave.

The pilgrimage was finally arranged, and, on the morning of Monday 29th May 2000, the family group, along with some friends, stood in silent respect to George Robert Schofield whilst a Scottish piper played the lament, 'The Flowers of the Forest'. As the sound of pipes faded away, a solitary figure walked into the cemetery. It was Des, George's best friend and the last person to see him alive. Des had heard of the visit but had initially been unable to join the group. However, at the last moment, he decided that it was too important a day to miss so had asked his son to drive him overnight to Holland from his home in the south of England.

The first thing Des did, when he found me, was to give me a hug and I wondered why he had hugged me! This was Des's first visit to George's grave and he gave us a first-hand story of how Dad had been killed. Des told me they'd been ordered to go out to enemy lines to 'take prisoners' and George, in his usual way, asked Des to go with him. They had fought their way through Normandy and Belgium together and had even celebrated my 1st birthday together before taking part in the Battles of Overloon and Venray. Their night patrol on 31st October 1944 had been a success, but whilst in No Man's Land, George had spotted a German patrol coming out of the woods south of Overloon. Whispering to his men to get down, he made sure they were safe, but a burst of machine-gun fire broke the silence and George lay mortally wounded, his head cradled in the arms of his best pal, Des. Realising the severity of his wounds, George's last words through stifled breath and tears were; 'I'll never see my baby. If you ever see him, give him a hug for me.' Then he died. And during that family visit to Venray in 1998, Des managed to pinpoint the spot where it had all happened and so the family, friends and myself made a poignant visit to the place where Dad had died all those years ago.

The Schofields and Almonds now have a family tradition thanks to George! Apparently, he loved a pint of Guinness, so every year, when possible, we visit George's grave and conduct the 'family Guinness ceremony' whereby everyone opens a can of Guinness, has a swig and then one can is poured on Dad's grave! My Dad has the greenest plot in the whole cemetery. Written at the base of Dad's grave is this simple inscription;

We have lost him; Heaven has found him. Jesus doeth all things well

Editor's Note:

The general requirement for inclusion in this book was that the Hampstead Pals must have visited the relative's grave and although the Hampstead Pals have been to Holland and visited the battlefield of Arnhem, we had never been to Venray. However, Ray has, for many years, been a popular member of the Hampstead Pals and travelled on many tours with us, often making professional-quality videos of the occasion. This, without doubt, qualifies him to tell us the moving story of how he found his dad.

We are proud to include it. God bless and thank you, George Robert Schofield.

Ray and son Paul remember...

Private Robert Adolphus SMITH
7th Battalion, The British West Indies Regiment
Killed in action 12th September 1917
Canada Farm Cemetery, Ypres

Found & commemorated at Canada Farm Cemetery by niece Beulah Coombs and
family, November 2015, who writes;

My parents and I immigrated from Jamaica to England in the mid-1950s. Every year,
on Remembrance Sunday, my mother would watch the TV broadcast of the Cenotaph
commemoration ceremony and would sigh and lament, 'My poor brother died in the
First World War'.

Being a child, this just seemed like a fairy tale to me and I took little notice. My parents returned to live in Jamaica in the seventies. I became interested in genealogy and when I visited my mother in 2007, in answer to my questions, she told me that in 1917, when she was aged three, she vaguely remembered her eldest brother, Robert, kissing her goodbye as he went off to England to go and fight for 'King and Country'. That was the last the family had seen of him. They were later informed that he had been killed. He was the son of James and Magiana Smith, of Good Hope, Kellits P.O., Jamaica. Unfortunately, I do not have a photo of him.

In 2008, on Remembrance Sunday, my daughter went to her temporary job and got talking to an older member of staff who happened to be a World War One historian. He informed her about the Commonwealth War Graves Commission (CWGC) website. With his assistance, she, amazingly, was able to find details about Uncle Robert, such as when he had died (12th September 1917), his age at the time (23), how he died (he had been wounded and taken to a 'dressing station') and where he died and was buried (Ypres in Belgium). There was even a picture of his Certificate of Commemoration displayed.

Back in Jamaica, my mother, then in her 90s, could hardly believe the news. 'After 91 years, I now know what happened to my brother,' she said, emotionally, looking at his Commemoration Certificate, (which also showed her parents' names), and at a picture of his inscribed headstone.

In August 2015, I made contact with Jonathan Nicholls of the Hampstead Pals via their website and he arranged to help my family visit the grave of Uncle Robert.

We were able to see further documents, including a war diary entry for the day he was killed. We learnt that he and other comrades, also soldiers in the 7th Battalion, British West Indies Regiment, perished from a German bombardment near Canada Farm, Elverdinge, where the soldiers had been working on 12th September 1917.

The 1st of November 2015 was a very momentous occasion for our family. After 98 years, thanks to Jon's assistance, we were finally able to be reunited with our uncle (and for some of us - great-uncle), Private Robert Smith.

Private Smith was one of many ordinary people who made the ultimate sacrifice and who gave their lives for the benefit of others. His story highlights to us the fact that people from across the British Empire and beyond, and not just those from the British mainland, fought and died in the World Wars.

The experience of travelling with the Hampstead Pals - Mick How was our driver - was absolutely fantastic from start to finish. Myself and two of my children, plus a brother and two of his daughters, were collected from my house in South London by Jon and Mick.

We immediately took to their kind, warm personalities and were made to feel extremely welcome. The minibus was spacious and very comfortable. Later in the day, and to our surprise, Jon opened a hamper of food - enough for 2 days, I would say - which automatically gave us the feeling of being with friends rather than just with an excursion company.

Following our pilgrimage to the cemetery, Jon and Mick took us into the historic town of Ypres where we had lunch, after which we visited the famous Menin Gate War Memorial. This is a huge monument inscribed with the names of about 55 thousand British and Commonwealth soldiers from the First World War, whose bodies were never recovered.

After 98 years, the fairy tale had come true.

Editor's Note:

Canada Farm Cemetery

This well-proportioned and attractive cemetery was designed by Sir Reginald Blomfield and Arthur James Scott Hutton. It is approximately five miles northwest of Ieper town centre, on the Elzendammestraat, a road leading from the Veurnseweg (N8) connecting Ieper to Elverdinge and on to Veurne. It can easily be located using the CWGC phone app.

Canada Farm Cemetery took its name from a farmhouse used as a dressing station during the 1917 'Passchendaele offensive' on this front. Most of the burials are of men who died at the dressing station between June and October 1917. There are now 909 First World War burials in the cemetery including the graves of 19 soldiers of the British West Indian Regiment, of which 17 are from the 7th Battalion. Among the many interesting graves of the opening day of the battle is that of Cpl James Llewellyn Davies VC, 13th Battalion Royal Welsh Fusiliers, who died from wounds sustained during the Welsh attack on Pilckem Ridge on 31 July. His citation in the London Gazette reads:

For most conspicuous bravery during an attack on the enemy's line, this non-commissioned officer pushed through our own barrage and single-handed attacked a machine gun emplacement, after several men had been killed in attempting to take it. He bayoneted one of the machine gun crew and brought in another man, together with the captured gun. Cpl Davies, although wounded, then led a bombing party to the assault of a defended house, and killed a sniper who was harassing his platoon. This gallant non-commissioned officer has since died of wounds received during the attack.

Before his death, the father-of-three wrote to his wife Elizabeth, stating; 'We are about to go over. Don't vex, as I hope to get through it all right, and if I do not, you will know that I died for my wife and children and for my King and country.'

The British West Indies Regiment. 'The Westies'

Following the outbreak of hostilities in 1914, many West Indians left the colonies to enlist in the army in the UK and were recruited into British regiments. In October and November 1915, many of the contingents were brought together at Seaford, West Sussex, England and were formed into the British West Indies Regiment (BWIR). The regiment's battalions saw service in France, Belgium, East Africa, Egypt, Palestine, Jordan, and Italy.

A total of 397 officers and 15,204 other ranks served in the BWIR. The regiment totalled twelve battalions and engaged in a number of roles and theatres. It was a 'volunteer' regiment, consisting of troops from the British colonies of the West Indies, which served on the Western Front and in the Middle East during the First World War.

The Regiment was awarded 5 DSOs, 9 MCs, 2 MBEs, 8 DCMs, 37 MMs and 49 Mentions in Dispatches. Although two battalions of the BWIR were involved in fighting in Palestine and Jordan against the Turkish army (where they sustained many casualties and honours), the War Office determined that Black colonial troops would not fight against Europeans. Consequently, most members of BWIR functioned in non-combat yet dangerous positions as labour battalions and were engaged in numerous support roles on the Western Front, including digging trenches, building roads and gun emplacements, acting as stretcher-bearers, loading ships and trains, and working in ammunition dumps. This work was often carried out within range of German artillery and snipers.

Of the total, 10,280 (66%) came from Jamaica, the third largest of the Caribbean Islands. In 1915, Britain's War Office, which had initially opposed recruitment of West Indian troops, agreed to accept volunteers from the West Indies.

The official records on the service of the British West Indies Regiment were destroyed during the Blitz, and much of the information written here has been gleaned from the Imperial War Museum. Altogether, 16,000 volunteered in the regiment and they served in the Middle Eastern, African and European theatres of the war. Over 1,500 perished, many through disease.

The 7ᵗʰ Battalion British West Indies Regiment

The 7th Battalion (6ᵗʰ Jamaican War Contingent - 34 officers, 1650 men) of the British West Indies Regiment, complete with its Alligator shoulder flash, sailed under the command of Capt. CD Arnold, from Jamaica on 31 May 1917, via Martinique, arriving to a tremendous welcome, with bands playing, in Brest, France on 18 June 1917.

From there, the battalion went to their final destination of 'International Corner' at Hazebrouck. As they left the train, they almost immediately came under shellfire. Whilst in Ypres Salient, they were almost constantly under shellfire while working at the railhead and ammunition dumps. On 12 September, the camp area was bombed and six men were killed including Private Robert Smith. They are all buried side by side at Canada Farm Cemetery, their graves maintained beautifully. 39 other men were also wounded during this bombardment. The battalion moved to Taranto at the end of December 1917 and lost a total of 189 men killed during the war.

Lance Corporal John STREET

1st Battalion, The King's Own Lancaster Regiment
Killed in action 10th April 1917
Arras Memorial, France

Commemorated by great-nephew Michael Jackson who writes;

When I was growing up, it was a family obligation to attend the Remembrance Service on the given Sunday in November. We had four family members who fought in the Great War and two in WW2. Out of the six, five returned, one was killed in action and one died in the mid-fifties, due to injuries received during WW2.

There was one person missing from our family group when we attended the ceremony at the Cenotaph in my home town of Runcorn in Cheshire. That person was my grandmother and I did not question why, but it was because of her brother John who never returned from France in the Great War. I was told she actually went to the unveiling of the Memorial in 1920 and the occasional service in the years to come. This was strange, as she would frequently walk past the Cross and go to the wall behind, on which granite plaques were embedded with the names of over four hundred townsfolk who had lost their lives in both conflicts.

Under the surnames beginning with "S" was the name of my great-uncle, Street J. There was no rank, regiment or date or death. My grandmother had hoped for many years that John was held as a prisoner of war and would one day walk back through the door in the regimented rows of the terraced houses in Runcorn that had, in common, the loss of so many of the town's menfolk. My grandmother passed away in 1976 yet much more sadness was to pass over her doorstep in her lifetime, as she experienced the early death of her husband (my grandad) in a wartime industrial accident and three out of her five children (my aunties) were to die in early life.

In civilian life, John Street was a staff member at Astmoor Tannery, Runcorn and was just 24 years old when he met his death on the 10th of April 1917, the second day of the bloody Battle of Arras. This is one of the main factors that started my interest in military history and research. Even today, there is still a mystery about John's service that I can't get to the bottom of.

His obituary says he went to France at Christmas 1915. Both the local newspapers carried the same wording but one carried a uniformed picture and the other a civilian picture. This was common to save distress to the family; one reporter would pass the details to the other paper's news desk and ensure that the photographs were returned to the family.

However, his service records don't survive but his Medal Index Card just shows entitlement to the Victory and British campaign medals. No entitlement to 14/15 Star and only shows a new army number and not the old regimental number to the King's Own Royal Lancaster Regiment.

We have a photograph of him in the South Lancashire (Prince of Wales Volunteers) pre-war economy uniform, with a leather belt, not webbing. The family talk is that he had a fiancée somewhere and went to France pre-1916 but I can find no trace of her, or of him serving in France. The records of the King's Own Royal Lancaster Regiment show that a block of numbers was issued in November 1916 and that he had reached the substantive rank of Lance Corporal in that regular army battalion in which he was killed. Had he been promoted during his training, it would have been unconfirmed. So where was Great-uncle John serving and what was he doing from October 1915 to November 1916? I have yet to find out.

I have gleaned information about his last action from the battalion, Brigade and Divisional war diaries, written at the time and very detailed. At the start of the battle on the 9th of April 1917, over 25,000 British soldiers had passed through the relative safety of the Arras tunnel network on their way to the front line. No such safety was afforded to the KORL who made their advance above ground, through the ruined villages of St-Laurent-Blangy and Athies, then on to Fampoux whilst under continuous shellfire from the enemy artillery. At one point, the battalion was briefly held up by uncut barbed wire but this was taken with little resistance. Many large and small artillery pieces, machine guns and mortars were captured and over 60 prisoners taken. Nevertheless, this successful breakthrough did not come cheap and the 12th Brigade diary, of which John's regiment was part, records the loss of 14 officers and 153 other ranks killed, wounded and missing.

Following the capture of the village of Fampoux during the afternoon of 9th April, the battalion was temporarily withdrawn from the line and primed for the attack on Roeux and the chemical works the following day. There was very heavy shelling of Fampoux but a reasonably quiet night was experienced by the battalion. On the morning of the 10th of April, L/Cpl Street answered the roll call and prepared for his last action. What was left of the battalion advanced around midday, alongside the railway embankment towards the heavily defended chemical works and railway station buildings of Roeux, which would take a month of hard fighting to subdue.

Although orders cancelling the attack had been issued, they failed to arrive in time and the depleted ranks of the 1st Battalion King's Own Lancaster Regiment advanced into a storm of machine-gun fire across a flat and open plain, devoid of any cover. What did those gallant men think of, in the agony of their hopeless advance? The diary records that the battalion lost 4 officers and 175 other ranks, killed wounded and missing. What price failure? L/Cpl John Street failed to answer the roll call on the 11th of April. He had answered a higher call. His body was never found or identified and his name is engraved on Bay 2 of the Arras Memorial. Due to the ferocity of the fighting, the ground on which he was killed was not cleared until the August of 1917 and during the heat of the summer, many bodies had become unidentifiable.

I have walked the ground over which the battalion advanced on that fateful day. The nearest possible burial place where John's body might be buried is the large

Brown's Copse Cemetery. Of the 2072 burials, the great majority of which are soldiers killed in the Battle of Arras 1917, 862 of the graves are unknown.

Within the walls of the beautifully maintained cemetery, which I have visited with the Hampstead Pals on many occasions, is a single headstone of an unknown soldier of the King's Own Royal Lancaster Regiment and I always place my hand on the stone and say 'hello.' In my mind, it is my great-uncle John. At peace…

Editor's Note:

I made these brief notes in 1990 shortly after the publication of *Cheerful Sacrifice* regarding **Brown's Copse Cemetery.** I recorded from experience that coaches should be reversed up the narrow lane to the cemetery as there is no turning point. It is even very tight to turn for cars.

This large cemetery can be seen in the fields from the level crossing at Roeux Station, although access is via the village of Fampoux. It stands in the middle of the old 'No Man's Land' over which a procession of 2nd Seaforth Highlanders, South Africans, Gordon Highlanders, King's Own Lancasters and many other battalions made unsuccessful attacks on the Roeux Station buildings and chemical works during the Battle of Arras in the spring of 1917. The cemetery is said to be named after a small copse nearby where Captain Charles Roydon Brown MC, 1st Essex, was killed in action on 14 April 1917 and is now believed to be buried. However, I personally believe it was so named after the Burial Officer of the 51st Highland Division, Lieutenant D Brown.

The bulk of the cemetery was formed in the summer of 1917 when the battlefield was cleared of the British dead who had been lying out on the plains in their hundreds since April. The Historian of the 51st Highland Division, Major FW Bewsher records that; 'Between Fampoux and Roeux Station, the British dead lay in swathes where they had been cut up in an attempt to exploit the success of 9th April against German machine gun rear guards,' and that 'Lieutenant Brown of the 8th Royal Scots and his men buried over 3000 dead between 9 April and 31st May.'

There are 2,929 graves of which 856 are unknown. By far, the majority of the graves are Scottish and include that of Lt. Donald Mackintosh VC (IIC49), 2nd Seaforth Highlanders, killed in action on 11th April 1917. The gallant attack of the 2nd Seaforth Highlanders took place on the 11th of April, from the sunken road at Fampoux, advancing to the chemical works at Roeux. 120 of the Seaforths killed on that day are buried in Brown's Copse Cemetery, which marked about as far as the majority of them got before they succumbed to the intense machine-gun fire from the chemical works.

Brown's Copse Cemetery typifies the lethality of the Arras fighting. 'The most savage infantry battle of the war' as described by Captain Cyril Falls, the official historian of the battle.

Here, in the heart of the Arras battlefield, lie the youngsters who made the supreme sacrifice, many in their first action. The legacy of the Somme battle is so evident because here lie the draftees, young volunteers and conscripts who replenished the depleted battalions of the Somme. The extreme youth of these soldiers strikes one to the heart, especially the graves of some of the South Africans; Private Matthew Campbell, aged 17, Private William Dunn, aged 17 and Private William Tranter, aged 16.

Brown's Copse Cemetery, Roeux. The village of Fampoux in the background.

Lieutenant Alexander Nigel TROTTER
2nd Battalion. The Royal Scots.
Killed in action 12 October 1914 aged 20 years.
Pont-Du-Hem Military Cemetery, La Gorgue, France.

Commemorated by the Hampstead Pals at Pont-Du-Hem Military Cemetery.

Jon Nicholls writes;

I am not in any way related to the subject of this unique 'Fragment of Remembrance' but I have long thought of Nigel Trotter and had wanted to visit his grave. Consequently, I have given myself 'editor's licence' to commemorate him here.

The lovely poem below was written by the mother of this young man, Lieutenant Nigel Trotter, who was killed near Bethune in France early in the Great War. In it, she recalls a family holiday they had spent in Picardie six years earlier when her son was a boy of 14.

I was given this poem to learn as an eleven-year-old pupil at Towcester Grammar School. It has had a major influence on my abiding interest in the Great War and is what love and remembrance are all about, especially as I had experienced a similar cycling holiday in Picardie with my own son when he was 14. A treasured memory.

The poem is a testament to a mother's love for her only son:

Picardie

There's a pathway through the forest in the Picardie I know,
A port where girls haul up the boats with men and fish in tow,
And the hills run down to the market town where the country women go.

And behind it is the village, and the coastline lies below,
And down the road, the dusty road, the carts ply to and fro
By the stately frieze of forest trees beyond the old Chateau.

There were three of us on bicycles upon the road that day;
You wore your coat of hunting green, and vanished down the way.
"Le petit chasseur, la mère et soeur!" we heard the women say.

You vanished as a speck of green among the shadows blue,
And children trudging up the hill stood still and called to you,
"Le petit chasseur, qui n'a pas peur," they laughed and called to you.

O boys, you wield the bayonet now and lift the soldier's load!
O girls, you've learnt to drive the plough and use the bullock-goad
But the hunter's lain, still unafraid, near the trodden Bethune road.

There's a pathway through the forest in the Picardie I know,
And O I'll dream and wander there; and poppy fields will glow;
And I'll watch the glare of the dusty air where the market wagons go.

Alys Fane Trotter

143

Nigel, as he was known, was born in London on 17th September 1894 to parents Alexander Pelham Trotter and his wife Alys Fane Trotter (née Keatinge). Nigel had an older sister, Gundred Eleanor Trotter (1889-1975), known as "Gunda", who was also born in London. He was educated at Packwood Haugh Preparatory School and then at Clifton College, Bristol, where he appears, aged 16, on the 1911 census.

He has a detailed entry in De Ruvigny's Roll of Honour which notes that whilst at Clifton College, he was a member of the Officer Training Corps, shot in the Bisley VIII, and was one of the best boxers in the school. The entry goes on to say that he was gazetted 2nd Lieut. 3rd Royal Scots, on 21st December 1912, and promoted to Lieut. on 9th July 1914.

He was appointed Transport Officer for the 3rd Battalion on the outbreak of war, leaving for France, aged 19, with a draft of 100 men, on 30th August 1914, sailing from Southampton on the SS Lake Michigan. A letter to his parents indicates that Nigel was in command of A Company on the day of his death, and he was first wounded in the chest before being shot again in the head as he was falling. His servant, Private W. Grant, wrote that he died at 11 pm.

The Roll of Honour records that Nigel was killed in action at La Fosse, near Vielle-Chapelle, 12 Oct. 1914, while engaged in attacking a wood strongly held by the enemy. The ground over which the British had to advance was intersected by small irrigation canals crossed by plank bridges, on which the officers and men offered a good target. Lieut. Trotter is believed to have been first hit while crossing one of these bridges, and after advancing three-quarters of a mile, fell with two more wounds. He was buried on the farm of Zelobes, near La Fosse, north of Bethune. His Coy. Commander, Capt. (now Major) F. C. Tanner, D.S.O., wrote: "Everyone is unanimous that Nigel died like a hero, and knowing him, I could not suppose it otherwise. I saw him under fire at the beginning of the action."

His mother wrote a book of poems after his death – 'Nigel and Other Verses', by Alys Fane Trotter (1862-1961), which was published in 1918. The frontispiece includes a photograph of her son.

Alys Fane Trotter

She was born Alys Fane Keatinge in Dublin in 1862. Her parents were Maurice Keatinge, a civil servant and Ellen Flora Keatinge, née Mayne, from Wiltshire. The family lived in London before Maurice retired when they went to live in the Manor

House at Teffont Evias, Wiltshire. Alys married Alexander Pelham Trotter on 25th June 1886 at the Parish Church of St James in Paddington, London.

They had two children - Alexander Nigel, who was born in London in 1894, and Gundred Eleanor Trotter born in1889. Alys lived to a grand age and died aged 99 in Wiltshire on 21st December 1961.

Pont-du-Hem Cemetery

The Commonwealth War Graves Commission says;

Pont-du-Hem was in German hands from mid-April to mid-September 1918. The cemetery was begun, in an apple orchard, in July 1915, and used until April 1918 by fighting units and Field Ambulances; these original burials are in Plots I, II and III, and Rows A and B of Plot IV. In April and May 1918, German burials were made in Plots III and IV. After the Armistice, 426 German graves were removed to other cemeteries; the Portuguese graves of 1917-1918 were removed to the Portuguese cemetery of Richebourg-L'Avoue and British graves were brought in from the surrounding battlefields and from smaller burial grounds. There are now over 1,500 1914-18 war casualties commemorated in this site. Of these, over half are unidentified and special memorials are erected to nine soldiers from the United Kingdom believed to be buried among them. Other special memorials record the names of 44 soldiers from the United Kingdom, two from Canada, two from Australia and one of the Royal Guernsey Light Infantry, buried in this or other cemeteries, whose graves were destroyed by shellfire, and of five Indian soldiers whose bodies were cremated. There are 107 German burials and 1 American. The cemetery covers an area of 6,433 square metres.

The Commission also records that Nigel Trotter's body was found and re-buried in this cemetery in September 1924. His body was identified by his badges and insignia.

Hampstead Pals at Pont-Du-Hem Military Cemetery in 2011
L-R Bill Gemmel, Anthony Stackhouse, Jon Nicholls & Mike Jackson

Captain Jack TURNER MC
8th attached 10th Battalion, The Royal Warwickshire
Regiment
Killed in action 22nd October 1918
St Aubert British Cemetery, France.

Commemorated at St Aubert Cemetery by family friend, Trevor Bettles,
Inspector, Metropolitan Police (Rtd), who writes;

My connection to Jack Turner is tenuous, in that he is the great-uncle to my first
serious girlfriend, Jane. The whole family remain dear friends, a friendship that has
endured for over 55 years!

Jack Turner was born 26th of March 1882, the eldest of four children born to John
Rootery Turner and his wife Emma, in Coggeshall, a small Essex town close to the old

Roman garrison town of Colchester. He was educated at Sir Robert Hitcham School, Coggeshall and later became a schoolteacher and subsequently taught in Hampstead, London (the spiritual home of the 'Hampstead Pals') and latterly, The National School, Coggeshall. Not much is known about his teaching career, but apparently, he gained a reputation in the local area as a sketch artist. Jack never married.

In October 1914, he enlisted into the ranks of the 8th Royal Warwickshire Regiment, (The Saltley College Company) in the nearby town of Colchester, where they were stationed prior to their and his departure to France in March 1915.

By November 1915, Jack had received his Commission to Second Lieutenant and whilst at the front and when not busy with the welfare of his men and other numerous duties required of a junior officer when not fighting the Germans, he became the 'unofficial' battalion artist, sketching the C.O, R.S.M and many of his fellow officers and men.

Having served in the ranks for a short time, his letters home reflected his concern for the privations of his men when in the line. He often marvelled at the relative luxuries of his fellow officers, because they had their own dugouts furnished with table and chairs, a stove and even the odd copy of Punch magazine! He waxed lyrical about the 'absolute luxury' of the Officers' Mess in some chateau in a relative area of safety when he himself was out of the line. However, he worried about - and never overlooked - the privations of his younger brother, Wilf, who at this time, had been captured by the Germans.

On 1st July 1916, the opening day of the Battle of the Somme, the 8th Royal Warwicks attacked the powerfully defended Quadrilateral Redoubt or 'Heidenkopf' near the village of Serre. Following that ill-fated action, his family had heard nothing from him and feared the worst but on the 8th of July, Jack finally managed to write to his family having completed the numerous onerous tasks that had befallen him as one of the few surviving officers of his battalion. He wrote;

> *Darlings,*
>
> *You should very humbly thank God – and you will – I scarcely know how to write to you – but the gist is that I am one of the officers who came through unscathed – don't believe the casualty lists… I hear I am among the wounded!*
> *– from one of the hottest and most awful battles in history. The 8th that you know, is a memory only. The C.O is dead, Hoskins, Fussell, Wareham, Proctor, Caddick, countless wounded… Washy, Boxer, James, Hands, Roy…*

Alas! Dear boys – God rest them! Meredith, Sammy, Chatham are wounded and away. F.F is unhurt. I have been in command of a company since. Though Coxon (who wasn't in it) has now relieved me.

We went over first – followed by crowds of famous regular regiments. The 8th were splendid – past imagination – The Regulars and their Generals cannot say enough for the dash and spirit of the onrush. But we were up against one of the most formidable positions of the whole line – and possibly the Prussian Guards and they met us with furious fire enfilading on both flanks, which, together with the terrific shelling, mowed us down like grass.

After two or three hours' advance, mostly crawling, I found myself in a big sort of crater trench and heard myself greeted by Captain Martin – "Bravo, Turner, come in, man – don't expose yourself – I can't afford to spare you." And there for hours, we consolidated a strong position with the help of a heterogeneous crowd of famous regulars who, having lost their own officers, clung to us... my own county among them. But our bombs gave out and, attacked on both sides by the enemy, we were slowly driven back. Later, I found myself with the remnants of a gallant Scots regiment and worked with their splendid Colonel, happily only slightly wounded.

Martin again joined us and we had orders to evacuate at dark – we had held on to a desperate position for over 12 hours. We had given up hope many times over and just gripped our revolvers or folded our arms and waited for the end. At nightfall, Captain Martin told me to get away with my dozen or so Warwicks... We crawled painfully over the shell-rent debris, sniped all the way. One man was hit. I came on to a wounded German. He begged for water. I tapped my empty water bottle; "Ich habe keine vasser," I said sadly. He smiled and murmured something which I would fain have caught... Oh! That awful journey. The dead and the dying, lying crawling along the ground... My God! Dear God!

In the early hours of Sunday morning, I was found asleep on a doorstep, in the desolate village nearby, by a Chaplain. He took me by the arm and made me sleep in an empty house. Next day, we got together our remains and came here, greeted with bands and cheering and the dear RAMC people have tried to kill us with kindness... Father Purdie and all my old friends. They made me go to silly "Curios" and cinemas and things, that I may not forget...

I feel as if I have just got through an awful illness...

> *This morning, dear Woods Hill, Lieut. RAMC took me out riding before breakfast, instructing me once again in the noble art which I may now require, for they talk about recommending me for my captaincy.*

> *But what is personal promotion at such a time?*

Wilson-Charge is C.O.

All my love

Yours truly, Jack.

PS – it is said that they didn't expect us to get through but only to hold the enemy while others got through.

Editor's note:

An interesting letter! The area described by Jack will be familiar to the Hampstead Pals who have visited the large Serre Road No 2 Cemetery on many occasions. It stands on the site of the Quadrilateral Redoubt, which was the objective of the 4th Division that day. To accomplish the task, the Division had been loaned two battalions from 48th Division, made up of Birmingham Territorials, the 6th and 8th Royal Warwicks, which in the first wave of the assault, advanced, with heavy loss, through the redoubt and a thousand yards beyond.

The 8th Royal Warwicks held the Quadrilateral against violent German counter-attacks throughout that hot summer's day until 7.30 pm, when what remained of the battalion withdrew to the village of Mailly-Maillet (where Jack met the Chaplain). The 8th Royal Warwicks, a Territorial battalion, lost 25 officers and 563 other ranks killed, missing or wounded. It was the worst day in the history of the battalion and indeed the British Army, which had suffered almost 60,000 casualties that day. The story of the 1st day on the Somme has been well documented elsewhere.

In his letter, Jack (who was in 'B' Company) tells us that during the day, they had lost the Colonel, Edgar Arthur Innes, who was a wine merchant by occupation and living at 93 Metchley Abbey Lane, Harborne, Birmingham. The 8th Battalion he commanded was a Territorial unit based at Aston in Birmingham and part of the 143rd South Midland Brigade. Having no known grave, his name is commemorated on the Thiepval Memorial.

The 'crowds of famous regular regiments' described by Jack would have been the 1st Battalion of the Rifle Brigade, the 1st Somerset Light Infantry and the 1st Hampshires and the 'Gallant Scots Regiment' would have been the 2nd Seaforth Highlanders.

It was due to his actions, on 1st July and thereafter, that Jack Turner was awarded the Military Cross in the New Year's Honours List, January 1917.

Whilst serving continually on the Western Front, in June 1918, Jack was awarded the Croix de Guerre and his correspondence to his family showed he was particularly proud of that decoration because he so admired the fortitude of the French civilians and the gallantry of their Armed Forces.

On 11th October 1918, Jack wrote his last letter to his sister Mary and it reveals that by this time, he was understandably war-weary but dared to imagine the end was in sight. 'Our Dear Boy's Grub' refers to his younger brother Wilf, a prisoner of war. Jack had just 11 days to live:

> *I am very glad you are home with dear Marg. But you mustn't worry about me or imagine all sorts of things without any particular reason. We are all – and you dear things, as much as we war- Campaigners in the mud and desolation - just absolutely in the hands of the bon Dieu – always. Please keep hold of that and don't upset yourselves until you have something to warrant it. I am worried about our Dear Boy's Grub. I expect it is pretty scanty. If you want any money for him, use some of that which I enclose and I'll gladly send some more. Please find cheque for £5. You can have more if you want it. It is not frightfully exciting to command a platoon after one has commanded a Company... Nonetheless, I have absolutely nothing to grouse about. C'est l'Armee and just think of the things I have to be grateful for. Don't worry on that score either.*
>
> *Fondest hugs, dearest one.*
>
> *Yours ever*
>
> *Jack*

On 22nd October 1918, Jack was killed in action, shot by a sniper, one of two officers from the 10th Royal Warwickshires killed that day, in the advance towards the village of Bermarin, to the north-east of Cambrai.

POSTSCRIPT from Trevor Bettles;

I think it fair to say that Jack was a devout Christian with high moral principles who considered it his God-given duty to stand up against the tyranny of the invading German hordes. It appears he was very attentive to the needs of his men and, in return, was much respected by them.

During his military service, he was a prolific writer of letters to his beloved family and they serve, with many others, as primary historical sources of the Great War. His family have commissioned a book of his surviving letters and circulated it to the members of the immediate and extended family.

In the 1980s, John Ralling - Jane's father and Jack's nephew - visited his grave and wrote the following poem;

It is a quiet country road
Avesnes to St Aubert
A mile or two of nothing much
Except, that halfway there
Runs off to North, between the fields,
A farmer's muddy track;
And there beneath a concrete cross
They buried Uncle Jack

Company Sergeant Major George WARD
2nd Battalion The Royal Lancaster Regiment
Killed in action 13 April 1915
Oxford Road Cemetery, Nr Ypres.

Commemorated at Oxford Road Cemetery by family friend Judith Rushby who
writes;

He was my maternal grandmother's fiancé…

My nan, Alice Robins, was born in Ravensthorpe, Northants on the 1st of
September 1893. The village is about halfway between Rugby and Northampton, and
really quite pretty. The older houses are built of that warm, honey-coloured stone that
is seen around that area. Cromwell's army came through the village the night before

the battle of Naseby and knocked all the heads off the statues in the church. This is probably the most exciting thing that ever happened there. Although very pretty, I must confess that I always found the area dull, especially the larger towns like Northampton, Kettering and Wellingborough.

My parents lived there for a couple of years in the 1980s, interestingly, on a lane that has some of the most expensive house prices in Northants - average house price £770k. I can remember being amused by the fact that all the old ladies in the village looked exactly like my nan, and the younger ones like my mum. My great-grandfather was a farm labourer and his wife looked after their large brood of children, 6 girls and 5 boys. They lived in a tiny cottage which is still there.

Nan left school around the age of 12 and became a maid at the big house in the next village. I think that this was Coton Manor and I also think that this was owned at one time by the Bryant family who were match manufacturers. It's just over a mile to Coton and takes around 25 minutes to walk. Nan was not allowed by her parents to live in, so she would make the journey very early every morning to light the fires in the Manor. I don't think that there was a school in Coton, as it was very small and so the children would make the reverse journey to the one that Nan made, to the school in Ravensthorpe.

Nan's eldest brother was called Joseph and he was born in 1890. His friend was called George Ward and he lived in Coton. He was born in about 1892 and was one of five boys. Uncle Joe and George both joined the army as boy soldiers – I'm not sure which year. They enlisted into the 2nd Battalion of the King's Own Royal Lancaster Regiment.

At some point, my nan and George became engaged. I like to think of them meeting in the lanes and pathways between the two settlements.

I know that my uncle and George were in the Channel Islands for a while and I also know that their regiment was in India when war broke out in 1914. They were recalled to England and then were sent to the Front – the regiment was there between January and November 1915.

George was killed on the 13th of April 1915. He now lies in Oxford Road Cemetery, just outside Ypres, in a row of graves from 1917. I understand that means he was probably buried out on the battlefield and was brought in a couple of years later when it was safe to do so. George was a Company Sergeant Major when he died and was only 23 years old. I guess that means that many more senior soldiers had died, but I also think that he must have been a good and well-respected soldier to have been given that rank. My uncle Joe died on the 8th of May 1915 just 25 days after his friend and is listed on the Menin Gate.

In the village of Guilsborough on the other side of Coton was an auxiliary hospital - I think that it was a fever hospital originally. The soldiers who were sent there would often walk through the surrounding villages when they were strong enough. My great-grandmother would call them in and give them tea when they walked past her cottage and her daughters would do their mending for them. And that is how my grandparents met. Grandpa had been in the Royal Horse Artillery and was sent home with a 'blighty'. He was seriously wounded and never returned to the Front.

My nan was still mourning her George and it was 6 years before Grandpa persuaded her to marry him. I think that a chicken farm was mentioned but it never materialised. They had four daughters and one son who was named George.

I have no pictures of George but I believe that he has descendants living in Nuneaton - maybe I'll track them down one day.

> *George Ward really did die so that we may live.*
> *I wouldn't be here now if he had survived.*
> *Goodnight and God bless you, George.*

Editor's Note:

Oxford Road is a deceptively large cemetery from the narrow entrance and really consists of two cemeteries with two definite sections. Its name originates from the road once running behind the support trenches. There are now 851 Commonwealth casualties of the First World War buried or commemorated in this cemetery. 297 of the burials are unidentified and special memorials commemorate three casualties known to have been buried in the cemetery, but whose graves could not be located.

The cemetery was designed by Sir Reginald Blomfield and the Hampstead Pals have been here on numerous occasions, mainly to visit the grave of the much-loved and outstanding English Cricketer, **Colin Blythe,** who was killed at the Battle of Passchendaele in November 1917 while serving with the 12th Battalion King's Own Yorkshire Light Infantry.

On the special day that Judith Rushby paid her moving tribute to George Ward, we were privileged to have with us the West Indies National U19 World-Cup-Winning Cricket Team Coach, *Graeme West,* who laid a wreath to the memory of Colin Blythe (Photo left). Also present was his proud father and ex-Metropolitan Police Detective Sergeant, John 'Dick' West (seated and mentioned in John Grieve's foreword).

Lance Corporal Arthur Frederick
WHITROD
8th Battalion, The Royal Fusiliers
Killed in action 7 July 1916
Thiepval Memorial

Commemorated at Ovillers Military Cemetery and Thiepval Memorial by great-niece
Eugenie Brooks, Sergeant, Metropolitan Police Royalty Protection Group (Rtd),
who writes;

This is the story of two cousins who died in the Great War; Roper and Arthur. I've
always known that my mum, who is now 90 and living in a care home, had lost two

uncles in the Great War. Thanks to my parents, I have a great love of history and know so much about these two men who I never met, but remember every day. I am named after both my great-grandmothers – Eugenie was my dad's granny and Caroline was my mum's granny. Let me tell you about them both, starting with a Kitchener's Volunteer, Arthur Frederick Whitrod.

Arthur was born in 1885 and was the youngest of three boys born to Harry and Caroline Whitrod who lived at 86 Carthew Road, Hammersmith. He had a younger sister called Ethel who I remember meeting when she was an old lady. Arthur's elder brothers were Albert – my grandad – and Walter. The 1911 census shows he was employed as a lather boy at a local barber's shop. He went to the local school in Brackenbury Road, which is still there, as is 86 Carthew Road.

There are a couple of strange coincidences now - when I first joined the Met Police, I was allocated a room at the Section House around the corner from Carthew Road in Goldhawk Road and I remember dealing with a road traffic accident outside Brackenbury Road school when I was posted to 6 Area Traffic at Alperton. Arthur's service number was 724. My warrant number is 7274. Out of all the numbers I could have been issued with…

On the 24th of August 1914, Arthur enlisted into the Army at Hammersmith recruiting office. He was given the regimental number of G/724 and joined the 8th (Service) Battalion of The Royal Fusiliers. A few days later he reported to Hounslow Heath to begin his initial training which took him to Colchester and Aldershot. On 31 May 1915, he embarked at Folkstone for service in France. Having landed in Boulogne, his battalion was in a local rest camp for a few days until it moved to the area of St Omer before moving onto the area of Steenwerke, Belgium. It was attached to the 48th Division for instruction on trench warfare and then, on 23 June 1915, took over an area of front-line trench in the Ploegsteert sector in front of the Chateau de la Hutte. From July to September 1915, the battalion served in and out of the line around Le Bizet, Houplines and Armentieres.

On 1st October 1915, he moved to Vermelles and entered the front line in this sector. The battalion was under almost constant shellfire for the next seven days. This was the Battle of Loos. For the whole of October, he was engaged in routine trench-holding duties under constant bombardment in the Vermelles sector when in the line. When out of the line, they were billeted in the mining village of Annequin. Christmas 1915 was spent in the front-line trenches at Givenchy. During this time, several German mines were detonated and there was much bombing activity in the vicinity.

For the first part of 1916, he was in and out of the trenches in various locations including Bethune, Arras and Vermelles. Then, in June 1916, the battalion travelled southward to the Somme. He was billeted at Vignacourt, then Fleselles and Frechencourt.

On the 1st of July 1916, the Battle of the Somme commenced. Arthur's battalion was held in reserve on the first day and moved forward into the line immediately northwest of Albert during the evening. After four nights in the frontline trenches, the battalion retired to Albert for one day's rest and was billeted in empty houses in the town.

On the 6th of July 1916, they were moved into forming up positions behind the frontline at Ovillers Post in preparation for an attack the following day. By this time, Arthur was a Lance Corporal and was 21 years old.

The objective of the battalion the following morning was the capture of the enemy front line and the village of Ovillers. The British artillery bombardment began at 06:45 am and was scheduled to lift at 08:30 am. However, a German counter-bombardment on the forming-up areas caused many casualties even before the attack went in. During the attack, which took place under intense enemy machine-gun fire, the first three German lines were taken and a foothold made in the village. However, the survivors couldn't hold these positions and had to fall back to the captured German second line. Casualties were heavy – only 160 men of the 800 committed to the attack managed to survive unscathed. The majority of those 640 casualties were wounded and missing but 160 soldiers of the 8th Royal Fusiliers had been killed in action. Arthur was last seen lying wounded in a shell hole but he was never found and so listed as missing. He is commemorated with pride on the Thiepval Memorial.

My mum can remember when she was a little girl, her granny Caroline – Arthur's mother – always being dressed in black as a sign of mourning. Granny Caroline had the picture of Arthur sitting in a chair in his uniform, (above) framed and on a table next to her chair. She used to touch the picture frame and say 'my poor boy, my poor lost boy.'

In 1984, I first travelled to France and the Somme area with my mum and dad. My dad's dad, Grandad John, had been a regular soldier prior to the outbreak of the Great War and had fought on the Somme as well as at the Battle of Mons and Le Cateau with the Old Contemptibles and we wanted to follow in his footsteps. However, our main reason to visit the Somme was to go to the Thiepval Memorial and lay some flowers from my Great Auntie Ethel for her young brother Arthur. We were the first from the family to make the journey and Great Auntie Ethel was delighted to hear that we had visited her beloved youngest brother and put flowers by his name from her.

We also visited Ovillers Military Cemetery which is situated in no man's land on the old battlefield. We stood looking over the ploughed field and I tried to imagine what hell Arthur saw when he went into action on the 7th of July 1916. There would have been dead bodies lying everywhere from the failed attacks of the previous 5 or so days, the murderous enemy machine-gun fire and mortars as well as the screams of his friends and colleagues on either side of him.

In that large cemetery are buried 3440 men of which 2480 are unidentified. I decided to adopt an unknown headstone as the final burial place of Arthur. After all, it is quite possible that he is one of the unknown soldiers buried there. I returned with friends and randomly picked an unknown headstone to the right of the steps. One friend played the Last Post on his bugle and another read a poem. I took some earth from the base of the headstone and put it carefully in a sealed pot. That earth was brought home to England and later, I scattered it on the grave of Arthur's sister, Ethel. She had always missed him and spoke of him when I visited her in her nursing home.

As far as I'm concerned, they are now reunited. I brought Arthur home to her and he is no longer missing as I always visit that grave when I'm out on the Somme. His story is told to all the groups I take to Thiepval, as I'm now a regular battlefield guide and it adds a personal touch with the story of my great-uncle Arthur and the effect his death had on his family.

If he had survived, I would have met him as an elderly gentleman as I remember his brother, my grandad, Albert.

The Great War took him away from me but he is never forgotten.

2nd Lieutenant Roper Henry WHITROD

4th Battalion, The King's (Liverpool) Regiment
Killed in action 28 May 1918
Gwalia Military Cemetery, Nr Poperinghe

Commemorated at Gwalia Military Cemetery by great-niece Eugenie Brooks,
Sergeant, Metropolitan Police Royalty Protection Group (Rtd), who writes;

My great-uncle, Roper Whitrod was born in October 1890 in Richmond, Surrey. His parents were Ramaiah and Eliza Whitrod and he had a brother called Ramaiah Charles and three sisters called Rose, Maude and Florrie. He was also cousin to Arthur Whitrod who was to be killed at the Battle of the Somme. Roper's dad, Ramaiah, was a Metropolitan police constable.

On 30th January 1905, Roper joined the Coldstream Guards as a boy soldier. He signed up in Stratford and I have seen his original attestation papers kept at Wellington Barracks, London. There's a lot of information on it. He was 14 years and 3 months old when he joined and his trade was a plumber's mate. He was 5'8" tall and weighed 84 lbs (6 stone in old money). He had a fresh complexion with brown hair and he belonged to the Church of England.

I have a family wedding picture, taken in December 1905, of Roper's sister Alice Maude and Roper is looking very smart in his uniform. In fact, he's about the only one who stood still for the cameraman as a lot of the others in the group are out of focus! He was in the UK for the first 18 months of his service and then was shipped off to Egypt on the 29th of September 1906 for 4 and a half years. On his return, he became a PT instructor based in Aldershot from about 31 December 1913.

When war broke out, as part of the BEF, the 1st Battalion Coldstream Guards was sent to France on 12 August 1914 – 8 days after the outbreak - until 21 September 1914 when he was wounded and badly shell-shocked with deafness and so returned to Aldershot where he served for 2 years training new recruits. During this time, he married his sweetheart Minnie Wesson in 1915 and they went on to have two children, a boy and a girl.

On 22 April 1917, he returned with the Guards to France. By late 1917, he was a sergeant. In May 1918, he returned to England to take a commission as a 2nd Lt in the 4th Battalion of The King's (Liverpool) Regiment (KLR). His name appears in the London Gazette dated 14th May 1918. In the war diary of the KLR, he is mentioned by name on 14th May 1918 as joining his regiment along with four other new young officers.

The next entry in the war diary with his name is dated 28 May 1918. It states 'killed on return journey from a working party by a shell, with 8 other ranks wounded.' The next day the entry reads, '2nd Lt R Whitrod was buried at 2.30 pm in Gwalia Military Cemetery near Poperinghe.' He was 28 years old.

His wife Minnie never remarried and was bitter about her loss. The inscription at the base of Roper's grave is unusual. Perhaps she knew of someone's husband who was kept behind the lines in a safe role and so survived, whereas her Roper had been killed in the last 6 months of the Great War. It reads;

'Better to die in the flower of youth, than to live at ease like the sheep'.

I have visited Great-uncle Roper many times and on the 100th anniversary of his death, I was honoured to lay a wreath in memory of him at the Menin Gate and recite the Ode of Remembrance. In St George's Church in Ypres, I have erected a brass plaque in his memory. I remember visiting Roper with the Hampstead Pals many years ago and us all sharing a beer with him by pouring beer at the base of his headstone. I'm sure he appreciated it!

Editor's note:

Gwalia Cemetery is a little bit of Britain with a touch of 'Welsh character' which brightens up the featureless surrounding farmlands. It lies about 2 miles NNE of Poperinge and was named after the nearby Gwalia Hop Farm, which later became a field hospital in 1917 and now contains 467 Commonwealth burials of the First World War. The cemetery was designed by Sir Reginald Blomfield and Noel Rew.

The cemetery was opened at the beginning of July 1917, in the period between the Battle of Messines and the Third Battle of Ypres.

Lance Corporal John Patrick HICKIE
15th Battalion, (The London Welsh) Royal Welch Fusiliers
Wounded at Pilckem Ridge, Belgium, 31st July 1917

A 'survivor' joyously commemorated at Pilckem Ridge Welsh Memorial by his son,
Major John Hickie MBE. Royal Artillery, who writes;

L/Cpl John Patrick Hickie was my father who, although a Lancastrian, enlisted into
'The London Welsh' on the 7th November 1914. He survived the war but died on 14th
March 1939 when I was only four years old, so I only have childhood memories of him.
His family could not relate stories or experiences from his wartime service so I can
only assume that like so many other veterans of The Great War, he never spoke about

what horrors he must have seen or experienced. In addition, the family have no photographs of him in uniform.

The London Welsh Battalion was formed in September 1914 at the Inns of Court, Holborn but left London in December to go to Llandudno and become part of 113 Brigade of the newly formed 38th (Welsh) Division. At the same time, they became the 15th Battalion (The London Welsh) Royal Welch Fusiliers. They maintained the title 'London Welsh' until they were disbanded in February 1918.

From my own research, based on my father's Record of Service together with the Histories of the London Welsh and 38th (Welsh) Division, I have been able to build up a picture of my father's war and what he might have experienced and endured. At Llandudno, on St David's Day, 1915, the Division was inspected by David Lloyd George. Training continued in Wales until August when the Division moved to Winchester and it was there on 29 November, that they were inspected by HM The Queen and her daughter, the Princess Mary. Finally, on 1st December, the Division marched overnight in pouring rain to Southampton where it embarked on 2nd December and sailed to Le Havre. The remainder of the year saw the battalion undergoing training at Merville and a turkey Christmas dinner paid for by the people of Wales.

In May 1916 at Laventie, the battalion had the honour of being the first in the Division to mount a raid on the German trenches, a raid that was regarded at General HQ as the third-best carried out by the British Army to date. In June, the London Welsh moved with the Division to join 2nd Corps and prepare for the Battle of the Somme. On 10th July, the Division was given the task of taking Mametz Wood. The horrors of the hand-to-hand fighting within that wood are beyond description with the battalion losing 12 officers and 251 other ranks.

In August, the battalion, along with 38th (Welsh) Division, returned to the Ypres Salient with long and weary periods of trench warfare varied by periods to the rear with football matches, sports and concerts, and, on St David's Day 1917, traditional ceremonies of 'The Leek'. At the end of June, the whole Division withdrew to the area of St Hilaire to prepare for the battle of Pilckem Ridge. A replica of the trenches and strong points had been prepared over which the Division trained. They returned to the line taking over The Canal Bank facing the Ridge.

On the night of 30th July 1917, the London Welsh reached its assembly position and, at 3.50 am on the 31st, the Division launched its attack behind an artillery creeping barrage. The London Welsh were on the left flank of the 38th (Welsh Division) supported on their left by the Guards Division. Having taken their final objective, a company was despatched to their right to an area known as Iron Cross where there was heavy hand-to-hand fighting. The present-day Welsh Dragon Memorial at Pilckem Ridge is at Iron Cross.

What part my father played in all or any of the above, what he experienced or saw, I shall never know. All I do know is that on 31st July 1917, on the first day of the Battle of Passchendaele, during the attack on Pilckem Ridge, he was wounded in the left foot and subsequently invalided out of the army. He never regained full use of his foot and received a pension until his death on 3 March 1939. I have walked the route of the London Welsh on 31st July from start point to final objective, then on to Iron Cross and again, shall never know at what point he was wounded.

As an addendum, in May 2016, on the Hampstead Pals' visit to the Welsh Memorial on Pilckem Ridge, Jon asked me to give a 'presentation' on my father and The London Welsh which I did based on the above. To finish off, I had brought some bottles of beer with which to toast The London Welsh.

What better or more appropriate beer could I have brought than 48 bottles of *London Pride*.

Editor's Note:

The author of this account was Major John Hickie MBE, (the son of the only 'survivor' featured in this book) who was a well-loved member of the Hampstead Pals and attended many Hampstead Pals Battlefield Tours. He did many, often humorous presentations, concerning soldiers of his own regiment, The Royal Artillery. He left this short contribution to the book which sadly, John did not live to see published.

He died peacefully on 14 July 2021 aged 87 years.

For you all love the screw-guns -- the screw-guns they all love you!
So when we call round with a few guns, o' course you will know what to do
Jest send in your Chief an' surrender -- it's worse if you fights or you runs:
You can go where you please, you can skid up the trees, but you don't get away from
the guns.

By Rudyard Kipling

Often sung with great 'gusto' by John Hickie, to the tune of 'The Eton Boating Song'.

CHAPTER 3

The Great Silence

9th SCOTTISH
MEMORIAL   2008

A Quiet Prayer

Two minutes silence digs deep
muddy trenches in the mind
where I fall to darkest shadow.
Endless dying groans, screams
drowned in death churned mud.

Then the gas constricting choke
amidst a panic for fumbled lost
masks. Bullets, shrapnel, gully
young lives into mother's tears, a
much loved photo of cherished
lover's memory, buried in mud.

For the great silence no ceremony
or poppy distracts our vision, no
trumpet sounds for quiet vigil just
a huge space between long ticks
of clock drown us in a timeless mud.

Police Constable Tim Savage, Metropolitan Police.

Sergeant John Joseph COUSINS MM
7th Battalion, The Bedfordshire Regiment
Born 29 January 1897 – Died 25 January 1988 aged 91 years
To France & Flanders with the Hampstead Pals May 1983

LEFT. 'Jack' Cousins in the studio 1915. 'Belligerent and ready for trouble' RIGHT.
Jack Cousins at Trônes Wood 1983 aged 86, 'Belligerent and ready for trouble'

Of the five British soldiers that the Hampstead Pals took to France in the early 1980s,
Jack Cousins was probably the most forthright. He had been involved in much close-
quarter fighting. He had fought in the renowned 18th (Eastern) Division – most feared
by the Germans - and came through all the major battles of the war without a scratch.

I had met him in the summer of 1982 when he had replied to a letter of 'appeal' I had published in the local Luton newspaper, looking for soldiers of the Great War.

Small and stocky, he had been a real 'handful' in his day. A farm labourer in his youth and, in his own words, 'just a village boy', who was born at the tiny hamlet of Trowley Bottom, Nr Flamstead in Hertfordshire, he was quiet and remarkably shy. At first, he hesitated to tell all. He carried an untold story. Many of them did. These were the boys who got the job done and came home.

This generation which had fought the Great War of 1914-18 had not yet faded in 1982. There were still many of them in our midst although they needed seeking out. Jack Cousins lived at 23 Stratford Road, Luton. When I met him, he had been a widower for five years. He was a great-grandfather too. Jack had been retired from local firm SKF some 20 years. During the 2nd World War, he had served as an ARP Warden.

He was a local man who had served in the 7th (Service) Battalion, the Bedfordshire Regiment during those traumatic years; one of Sir Ivor Maxse's men. He had declined our initial invitation to go back to the battlefields with the Hampstead Pals. 'I have too many bad memories,' he said. He didn't want the nightmares to start again. A telephone call from him some months later would change that. 'Does your invitation still stand?' He wanted to lay the ghosts before his time was up. When old soldiers mix with young police officers on the battlefields, the mixture is heady, emotional and sometimes hilarious. The stories would flow.

Jack had won the MM on the Somme at Thiepval on 26-27 September 1916. We wanted to hear about it. He wouldn't talk about that here. In France, it would be different. He liked his Guinness. He also drank whisky.

There is one episode in his story of the war that will stay with me forever and that was the day we took Jack Cousins back to Thiepval and the Schwaben Redoubt.

The night before the 18th Division attack on the 26th of September, Sir Ivor Maxse, had issued this confident order;

'The 180th Regiment of Wurtemburgers have withstood attacks on Thiepval for two years, but the 18th Division will take it tomorrow.'

Jack was there. We took him to the Mill Road Cemetery, where he recognised some of the names of the Bedfords on the flat headstones. This is what he said;

'I was lucky – you couldn't go by the book. You have to change your ideas.

It's either you or them. Don't wait to be asked - get stuck in - I always did.

We were advancing along this German trench. We never attacked Thiepval and the Schwaben Redoubt frontally; we did it from the flank, so we had to shoot our way along the trenches. I was a Lewis gunner and I had my finger on the trigger when a group of German soldiers with rifles in their hands came around the corner in front of us. There was no time to ask questions. I fired first and killed them. The Lewis gun was a wonderful weapon which fired a stream of bullets. I had trained myself to fire it in short bursts. After I had shot this lot, we advanced around the enclave and I threw a Mills Bomb down the steps of a dugout. I heard it explode and I went down the steps. There was this very young German sitting on the edge of his bunk bed and every time he breathed, the blood squirted from a hole in his chest. He said to me 'vasser, vasser', so I gave him a drink of water from my water bottle and the water squirted straight out of the hole in his chest. Well, he only lasted a minute and just keeled over and died. He had taken out his family photos from his pocket and was looking at them. I took those, and his prayer book; why, I don't know 'cos I couldn't read German.

There is one other thing. It's something I've kept to myself and never told anyone else. I am not proud to say that further along the trench, a large group of 12 or so Germans threw up their arms and surrendered. 'Kamerad, Kamerad' they said. I gave them the full magazine. I killed them all. You couldn't trust them, you see. I regret that now, of course. They were only doing their duty too. But it was them or us. That's what they gave me a Military Medal for…

I suppose today it's classed as murder.'

The C.O., Lt Col. George Dominic PRICE, CMG of the 7th (S) Battalion The Bedfordshire Regiment, left a stirring report of the action at Thiepval. He had decided to attack the untaken portion of Thiepval, i.e. the north-western part of the village. It was to be 'Death or Glory'. He wrote;

'The courage, resolution & endurance displayed by all ranks was quite wonderful. They were out to kill and the Battlefield is a witness that they carried out to the full their intentions. Even when the battalion had been relieved by the R.W.K. and volunteers were called for in the event of a counter-attack being successful on the ground they had so dearly won the preceding day, every man declared his willingness to return at once if needed.'

Hero returns to the Somme

CHAMPAGNE and tears were flowing when war veteran Jack Cousins returned to the Somme battlefields to a hero's welcome.

Sixty-five years had passed, but again Jack, now aged 86, found himself scraping the familiar mud off his boots.

The great grandfather — decorated with the Military Medal for bravery in 1916 — was last week taken on a nostalgic journey back to the battlefields by a "troop" of policemen.

Back home in Stratford Road, Luton, Jack, a widower, said "I have never experienced such hospitality before. Everyone wanted to buy me drinks.

"I stood in the fields and thought it's over 65 years since I stood here, and the present and past became merged.

"I laid a poppy wreath on

the monument to our Division and tears were rolling down my face.

"Then I got back into the minibus with the boys and they gave me a whisky and made me laugh."

Jack was taken to stay in the Somme village of Albert by his police sergeant friend, Jonathan Nicholls.

Mr Nicholls who lives in Hemel Hempstead and a dozen of his police officers are members of the Western Front Association and regularly take war veterans on remembrance trips to the Somme.

On his last night Jack was given a bottle of champagne by another war veteran.

Every day he visited the military cemeteries and saw the graves of soldiers who were with him in the Bedfordshire Regiment, where he was a sergeant and machine gunner.

Jack Cousins . . . present and past became merged

The battalion war diary recorded;

'During this action, 36 prisoners were taken & about 100 Germans killed by rifle fire & bayonets. This action, though apparently small, was of the utmost importance as without the whole of the Village of Thiepval & the trenches surrounding it being captured, the whole Line of Attack was held up. So, to the 7th Bedfords (especially C & D Coys) belongs the honour & glory of the final destruction of one of the Germans' strongest positions & one which they had boasted could never be taken. The morale of the battalion was extremely high. The men fought with determination & skill, gained all their allotted objectives, & received the highest praise from their Brigadier, Divisional Commander, Corps Commander, Army Commander & especially congratulated by the G.O.C., Sir D. Haig.'

It was an emotional moment for Jack when he produced a letter for us that he had written to his parents following the capture of Thiepval and the Schwaben Redoubt. Jack had been in action on the fateful 1st day on the Somme, 1st July 1916 and had seen many of his pals killed in the attack on Pommiers Redoubt, near Montauban. He had written;

> *"Dear Mum & Dad, I am pleased to tell you my old gun has done its bit; I have had my revenge for July 1st, I have had my share in the business."*

The business he was talking about was, of course, *killing*. The fight for Thiepval and Schwaben Redoubt was one of the great turning points of the War. The 18th Division had conquered a fearsome enemy which had defeated all previous attempts to take it since 1914. Sir Ivor Maxse wrote;

> 'I am convinced that, if the complete story is ever written of what our men accomplished in the way of hand-to-hand encounters from the outbreak of the Battle of the Somme until Thiepval and Schwaben were captured, their achievement will bear comparison with any similar feat of arms in the war.'

Jack wrote to me after that emotional tour in 1983; I still have his letter...

> 'Nowadays we are told, "Don't go living in the past. The present and the future are more important." Maybe, but to think back and being able to talk to some of your own age group and listening to them is a memory I shall treasure forever. When the last post sounds, I will have no regrets. I have met some wonderful people and it's made my life happy. Thanks to you all for your efforts to bring happiness, understanding and caring for those of us who fought that war and may the future bring the satisfaction of knowing that you have, in the past, done a good job. The Hampstead Pals gave me something that I shall cherish always. I think about it when I go to bed and it's on my mind in the morning. I have told all my relatives and friends the depth of gratitude I owe to you all for the care and attention you gave me during the five days I was in your company.
>
> The laughter still rings in my ears.'

Editor's Note:

In the capture of Thiepval, the 54th Infantry Brigade, of which the 7th Beds were part, lost 47 officers and 937 men killed, wounded or missing. German casualties exceeded 4,000.

The official history itself devotes five pages to the fight for Thiepval and concludes that;

> '54th Brigade had done all that could be expected in a fight where the prowess of the individual soldier largely decided the issue. For the most part, the enemy fought to the death; he was only to be overcome by desperate courage, skill-at-arms and the enterprise of small groups of men often led by privates after officers and NCOs had been killed or wounded.'

'The prowess of the individual soldier largely decided the issue'
Well done, Jack Cousins!

Further Reading about Jack Cousins MM;
The First Day on the Somme. Martin Middlebrook. (Allen Lane 1971)
Cheerful Sacrifice. The Battle of Arras 1917 Jonathan Nicholls. (Pen & Sword 1990)

Company Sergeant Major William 'Bill' HAY

9th (Highlanders) The Royal Scots
Born 16 January 1895 – Died 1 December 1985 aged 90 years
To France & Flanders with the Hampstead Pals 1980 –1985

LEFT. Bill Hay in 1915
RIGHT. Bill Hay lays a poppy wreath in memory of his fallen comrades at the Menin Gate 8 pm Last Post Ceremony in September 1980. Note that the wreath is homemade and bears an actual helmet badge of the Metropolitan Police. Within 5 minutes of the ceremony finishing, the wreath was stolen.

Extracts from the Eulogy given by Jonathan Nicholls to Bill Hay at his ashes-placing ceremony at Sanctuary Wood Cemetery on 5 March 1986.
'An old soldier's last wish carried out. A promise kept. A duty done'

Bill Hay was born in Edinburgh on 16 January 1895, the son of a coachbuilder and one of ten children. He left Torphichen St School at the age of 14 years to follow his father's trade. He yearned for the adventure of Army life, however, and, much to the annoyance of his father and distress of his mother, he enlisted in the 3rd Battalion Argyll and Sutherland Highlanders, a reserve battalion, then stationed in Stirling Castle. His father, not wanting him to be a soldier, probably foreseeing the outbreak of a major European war, actually 'bought' his son out of the army.

Before the outbreak of war on the 4th August 1914, Bill was already back, however, this time as a Territorial or 'part-time' soldier in the 9th Battalion, The Royal Scots. What had attracted young Bill was the fact this battalion was the only battalion of the Royal Scots to wear the kilt. Nicknamed the 'Dandy Ninth', they were Edinburgh's own proud battalion, the majority of men being natives of Edinburgh.

The 9th Royal Scots were the first Edinburgh battalion to go to the front. As early as November 1914, the battalion had been under orders but these were cancelled since it could not be spared at that time from coastal defence duties. At last, much to the excitement of young Bill, just 19 years old, the unit left Edinburgh on the 23rd of February 1915 and sailed from Southampton on the SS Inventor, a ship remembered with much affection by Bill. Arriving in Le Havre on 26 February, the battalion moved straight to the front as part of the 81st Infantry Brigade attached to the 27th Division. Bill wrote a hurried postcard to his mother, which must have worried her. 'Dear Mother, we have arrived in France safely and are going straight to the firing line.'

As soon as the battalion arrived at the front, it was introduced to the discomforts of trench warfare being sent to a very nasty part of the line just south of the town of Ypres at St Eloi. For the next few weeks, the 9th Royal Scots spent time in and out of the line around Ypres being billeted at Dickebush and Vlamertinghe, legendary places always mentioned by Bill.

On 22 April 1915, the German Army, determined to capture the town of Ypres and break through to the channel ports, launched a ferocious attack on the town; this was known as the Second Battle of Ypres. This attack was preluded by the first use of poison gas in the history of warfare.

Terrified by the advent of this fearsome new weapon, French Zouave troops, holding the line to the northeast of Ypres, fled in panic. The road to Ypres was open. Fortunately for the Allies, the Germans hesitated in order for the gas to disperse. This enabled fresh soldiers to be thrown into the line to block the gap. The Canadians came straight into action at St Julian and fought with tremendous courage and at great loss, temporarily stemming the German advance.

The 9th Royal Scots, by this time, were temporarily billeted in huts at Vlamertinghe, where they expected to have four days rest but on the morning of 22 April, shells rained down on Ypres, which still retained a large proportion of its civilian population, and, in fear and panic, the Belgians streamed down the road to Poperinghe. At nearby Vlamertinghe, the Royal Scots watched the pall of smoke and dust that lay over Ypres. Soon, the eastern sky was bright with the flames of burning buildings. At 7 pm on the 22nd, orders were received for the 9th Royal Scots to move forward and the men marched off in the direction of Ypres. At midnight, after a fast and tiring march, the battalion arrived in Ypres and found the town a mass of burning buildings, smoke and flame. In Indian file, with 50 yards between platoons, The Royal Scots hurried through the inferno, sticking close to the sides of ruined houses. The troops, by some miracle, passed through the town and out of the Menin Gate without a casualty. Upon leaving the Menin Gate, they took the left fork in the road and marched to Potize Wood, where they dug in.

The battalion remained in the wood until 12 noon the following day, when they were ordered to advance alongside the 2nd Duke of Cornwall's Light Infantry, their task being to plug the gap on the left of the Canadians. Advancing, they crossed the Ypres-St Julian Road and pressed on towards Pilckem Ridge, where they advanced up a long gentle slope. When they topped the rise, they immediately came under machine-gun fire from the opposite ridge, the enemy being there in force. The Royal Scots pluckily fixed bayonets and descended the slope under fire. They then took shelter for a two-hour period alongside a road. Then came the order to advance. The Royal Scots stood up and charged up the slope towards the enemy. At the sight of the kilted Jocks with bayonets flashing, the Germans turned and ran. They were already aware of the fighting reputation of the 'Ladies from hell'.

Hampstead & Highgate
EXPRESS

No. 6,532   FRIDAY, MARCH 14, 1986

War veteran's ashes scattered on battlefield

BILLY Hay's last wish was that his ashes should be sprinkled on the battlefield in Belgium where he fought as a young man.

And so last week a group of 15 policemen from Hampstead station, who looked after Bill in his later years, made the trip to Sanctuary Wood in Belgium, where he fought in 1915 with the Ninth Battalion of the Royal Scottish Regiment.

Bill, who lived in Solent Road, West Hampstead, died on December 1, 1985. He would have been 90 this year. He had taken part in the battle of the Somme and was wounded in 1917 at the Battle of Arras. He was also present the first time that

gas was used in combat.

In March 1918 Bill was captured by the Germans, but while he was a prisoner of war he managed to escape twice. Each time he was recaptured.

Donald Hay, Bill's son, accompanied the police group and a representation from the Royal British Legion also attended the battlefield outside Ypres.

Sergeant Jonathan Nicholls, from Hampstead Police Station, said: "Bill sent us a letter before he died which said that he would like his ashes to be scattered among those of his young chums who fought so bravely for their country."

After this brief but important encounter, the Dandy Ninth were withdrawn to Potize Wood, a place where Bill requested the Pals to take him on his first visit. On 24-25 April, they were back in the line at St Julian with the Canadians. At nightfall on the 27 April, they were relieved and marched to the more peaceful vicinity of Sanctuary Wood, and there, dug trenches awaiting the German attack which they expected at any time to come down the Menin Road. During this period of 22-29 April, the battalion had suffered casualties to 9 officers and 100 other ranks.

For the next three weeks, the battalion was in position in Sanctuary Wood, very near here, in trenches just in front of the land on which this cemetery stands. On the 8th of May, the expected attack came. The trenches to the north of the Menin Road were subjected to a terrific bombardment which smashed in the parapets and buried whole sections of defenders. Then the terrible fire swept south of the Menin Road and into the trenches of the 9th Royal Scots. From their uncomfortable positions, the battalion could see the Germans attacking to the north of the road. Then the enemy broke through to the south of the road, the Gloucestershire Regiment having been overcome. Suddenly, from along the Menin Road, came another battalion of the Royal Scots with bayonets fixed. They charged the enemy and drove them back. These were the regulars of the 1st Battalion and soon they had filled the gap alongside the 9th

Battalion. For the first time in their history, two sister battalions of Royal Scots were in the line side by side.

Here, both battalions endured the shellfire and fought off numerous German attacks until 24 May when they were relieved. The heavy shell fire and gas had caused severe casualties in the ranks of the 9th Royal Scots and among those young lads killed are the graves that lie here in Sanctuary Wood cemetery.

Most of these soldiers buried in this plot here were known personally to Bill. Most were in his platoon. 'Jocky' Jack was his closest friend; he had been killed on 17 May 1915 and died in Bill's arms. The majority of the 9th Royal Scots killed near here received no burial at all. Their names are on the Menin Gate Memorial to the Missing.

After this traumatic introduction to modern warfare, Bill saw much action in other parts of France and Belgium, including the Battle of Loos in September 1915. On 1st March 1916, the 9th Royal Scots were transferred to 154 Brigade of the famous 51st (Highland) Division. In August 1916, Bill saw action at the Battle of the Somme when he found himself in action at the notorious High Wood, and, in the November, took part in the last great battle of the Somme, the capture of Beaumont Hamel.

The following 9th April 1917, Bill was wounded on the first day of the Battle of Arras, on the flanks of the Vimy Ridge, near the village of Roclincourt. It was a wound that almost cost him the sight of his left eye and would cause him problems for the rest of his long life. This, however, would not keep him out of action for long and in July and August 1917, he was in action at the Battle of Passchendaele - not far from this spot - on the Frezenberg Ridge.

By this time and at the young age of 22, he was a Company Sergeant Major and had been in the war for three long years. In the spring of 1918, Bill's luck finally ran out when he was captured in action on the banks of the St Quentin Canal while holding up hordes of advancing Germans with a Vickers gun. He was lucky. After that, he spent nine miserable months in captivity, escaping twice and being recaptured.

Throughout his adventurous but harrowing service to his country, he never lost the amazing and characteristic sense of humour that was so typical of the man. Many remember his often-repeated stories, some tragic, but mainly humorous. Like the time, soon after being captured, a German soldier tried to lift his kilt in an attempt to solve a common but universal mystery and was soundly kicked on the shins by a bad-tempered Bill, for which Bill took a severe battering from his guards.

Then, there was 'the winning' of the boxing gloves in Armentieres in 1915, which belonged to the world heavyweight champion, Georges Carpentier and how the battalion was paraded next morning and the culprits ordered to 'step forward'. Bill's laughter still resounds when he remembers standing alongside his mate Alec Wright on that parade, each with a boxing glove stuffed under his tunic. (They were later put back in their original cabinet that night).

All of his stories featured his friends, true and faithful comrades with whom he shared the rigours of the trenches. These pals, who became familiar names to all of us, 'Jocky' Jack, Jimmy Pearson, Alec Wright, 'Porky' Flynn, 'Tolie' Davidson and his beloved company commander, Pat Blair, never came back. They were denied the chance to live a long and happy life. Denied the chance to Love. Denied the chance to see their children grow. They are here. On the old Western Front. Mainly forgotten by today's generation. They will always be here, buried near where they fell, fighting for a better world for us.

It is here at Sanctuary Wood, which featured so strongly in the British Army's valiant defence of Ypres, a town close to Bill's heart, that Bill asked his beloved Hampstead Pals - whom he always likened to his old army pals - to return and scatter his ashes. I would like to quote to you an extract from a letter to me, dated 9 July 1984;

'How the hell I came through all that is beyond me. But I'm very much alive today although a little weary. I have some fine friends and erstwhile comrades of West Hampstead Police. To them, I am truly thankful. We that are left must never forget the debt we owe to the thousands of young men who gave their all that we should live in peace. God help me I am 89. How I am here, I'll never know. I must have a guardian angel looking after me. After the episode at the Chemical Works in April 1917, when we got a right old bashing and the rest of my pals were killed, I was left sadly alone. How I hate to be alone. When I get my checks, I want to be scattered among my youthful chums, where I could have been. Memories, memories; the finest young men who ever breathed, my generation.'

Bill Hay chooses his 'place' in 1980

Bill Hay was a socialist. But his socialism was of a simple kind. Not born of hate but born of the trenches. He had also known the 'thirties and didn't want to see it again.' He remembered the dole queues and the hardships of those days.

"Would you like to go back to France, to the old action spots?" I asked Bill Hay. (I was on night duty and reposing in his armchair at his little flat in Solent Road). 'I am not sure' he replied. 'There are too many bad memories. But I would love to see my pals again.' His gentle Edinburgh burr made my eyes heavy. It was 2 am. He had waited up for me. He made me a cheese and pickle sandwich and poured me a generous 'Famous Grouse.' I was Duty Officer that Sunday night. The Inspector had gone sick. Bill wanted to talk about the war. 'I left my young pals there. They will always be part of me. Now, in the winter of my life, I think I would like to go.'

Throughout a life of hard work as a coachbuilder, milkman and ARP in the Second World War, when he was bombed out of his West Hampstead home in the Blitz while struggling to bring up a young family and ably supported by his devoted wife Isa, Bill never forgot the pals he left in Flanders fields. He was 86 when we first brought him back to the old action spots.

It was Bill's dearest wish that his son Donald should accompany us on his final visit. He came with us and, from money Bill had put aside for the occasion, purchased several bottles of whisky to toast his father. He wore his father's medals too. Bill's favourite tipple was a 'Rusty Nail' a powerful concoction of Whisky and Drambuie, so we duly anointed his 'grave' with a generous measure.

The Hampstead Pals were honoured to organise this sad but unique occasion. We promised to always return here in the years to come, to this beautiful and sacred spot at Sanctuary Wood Cemetery and remember Bill's generation that died here.

We have kept that promise.

Grandson Alastair Hay makes the long journey from New Zealand to join the
Hampstead Pals in May 2016

Further Reading about Bill Hay

Cheerful Sacrifice. The Battle of Arras 1917: Jonathan Nicholls. (Pen & Sword 1990)

Somme: Lyn Macdonald 1996

Great War Portraits: Keith Collman 2009

Note

Bill returned to the battlefields with the Hampstead Pals four times from 1980 to 1985. He was also a veteran member of the newly-founded Western Front Association. In May 2015, the Hampstead Pals held a ceremony at Sanctuary Wood Cemetery in memory of Bill Hay and an engraved Scottish granite plaque was placed on the headstone of 'Jocky' Jack. (Private Frank Cotton Jack aged 21).

It was duly anointed with a generous 'Rusty Nail'.

Private William 'Bill' PARTRIDGE

Sergeant, 1/7th Middlesex Regiment
2nd Lt. 19th Battalion Durham Light Infantry
2nd Lt. Gunner/Observer, 4 Squadron Royal Air Force
Born 7th October 1893 - Died 19th April 1986 aged 93 years
To France & Flanders with the Hampstead Pals 1985

LEFT. Bill with his wife Ida 1918
RIGHT. Bill at Gommecourt with the Pals 1985
Photos above and below courtesy of Keith Collman

Keith Collman writes;

I first met Bill in August 1984 when I was invited to join a trip to the old Western Front with twenty other veterans of WW1. Spending a week in his company, I learnt he had quite a war. On return from the trip, I would visit Bill at his maisonette in Hemel Hempstead, where he lived alone, his wife Ida having died in 1978. He would offer a brew and a piece of cake, which normally came in two slices, one thick, the other thin. We would then chat until we were in near-complete darkness; he only stopped to listen to the racing results on his radio.

Born 7th October 1893 in North London into a working-class family, he was an Arsenal supporter from 1910. In 1912, he emigrated to Canada, looking for adventure. The journey, lasting 11 days and covering 800 miles by train at a cost of £7, was paid for by his father. In 1914, he returned to visit his family, during which time war had been declared. He enlisted into the 1/7th Middlesex Regiment at Hornsey Drill Hall. Issued with pack and rifle, the battalion set sail to Gibraltar in September 1914 for training and garrison duty. The regular soldiers were amazed to see these new recruits dressed in sports jackets and straw boaters. They returned to the UK in February 1915, mobilised and prepared for embarkation to France.

The battalion arrived in France in March 1915, their first action being at Fromelles, The Battle of Aubers Ridge, May 1915. In the trenches, they formed a 'mucking-in school,' consisting of four friends who shared their parcels from home. Alf Davies was one. Bill and Alf survived the war but the other two were killed in September 1916 on the Somme.

In 1985, I found Alf Davies living in Bournemouth and arranged for Bill to visit. Alf was nursing his wife Hazel at the time and was somewhat distracted at first but after a few beers, he warmed to the occasion and chatted to Bill as if they were sitting on a fire-step back in the trenches, remembering names and experiences as if was yesterday. After leaving Alf, we sat on the seafront, where Bill had a sudden angina attack. I got him home alive, thank God!

Bill served in the trenches throughout 1915; in May 1916, as part of the 56th (1st London) Division, he arrived at Hébuterne, a small village just south of Gommecourt Wood, in the northern sector of the Somme battlefield. Prior to the battle, Bill watched the bombardment of the German positions from his parapet; 'It was so intense I could not believe how anything could be left alive!' But they were. In the early hours of the 1st July 1916, the first day of the battle, Bill's battalion assembled in reserve trenches under continuous shellfire. Bill was wounded in the head and shoulder and sent back to a dressing station and then home to the UK. He returned to the Somme six weeks later. Having survived the Somme and the winter, he took part on the first day of the Battle of Arras, 9th April 1917.

After the battle, Bill was recommended for officer training and he was commissioned on 25th September 1917 into the Durham Light Infantry. On 21st November 1917, he was drafted to the 19th Battalion in the Ypres Salient where he commanded a platoon of ex-miners, tough men from the northeast of England. He remembered, 'I couldn't understand a word they said!'

During a rest period out of the line, Bill was dining with a fellow officer when they met two Royal Air Force officers who invited them back to their living quarters. Bill was amazed to see their facilities; 'Bloody hell! Sheets, you lucky bastards, you've got it made, that's what I want, bloody right.' He went straight to his Colonel and requested a transfer to the Royal Air Force. At first, he was refused but later, the Colonel relented and Bill's application was accepted. Bill wrote to his future wife Ida about the transfer, and she replied, 'What do you know about flying?' 'Nothing', replied Bill, 'but I've seen their beds. I've lived in holes for four years. There's no gas up there; all I've got to do is sit in the back seat and keep the flies off the driver. I haven't got to fly the bloody thing!'

In June 1918, he returned to England and joined the Royal Air Force as an Observer/Gunner flying RE8s. Whilst on leave, he married Ida Prosser in Edmonton.

He joined No 4 Squadron in France and started flying over the very trenches he had recently left. But his war ended in October 1918 when out on patrol, his young pilot passed a note to Bill; 'Juice is short!' Bill replied, 'How short?' 'Ten minutes!' replied his pilot. As they headed towards their airfield, a thick ground mist sprang up, and they couldn't see a thing! They just avoided a church steeple. Bill fired several flares, then they spotted a gap in the mist and headed downwards. The next thing Bill remembered was waking up in hospital. Whilst he was convalescing from his injuries, the war ended.

Back in civvy life, Bill worked for the Inland Revenue in North London where Tottenham Hotspur players would come into his tax office. They were obviously overpaid. During WW2, he tried to enlist in the Middlesex Regiment and then the RAF but the Inland Revenue would not release him.

On his retirement, he had a heart attack but lived for almost another 30 more years, defying his doctor's advice to quit smoking. Bill recalled the comradeship of the trenches under such hardships; 'I would not have missed it for the world.' He hated being referred to as a hero. 'I was just one of the lads; I did what everyone did!'

Alf Razzell and Bill Partridge 'Stand to' at Bullecourt 1985

Further Reading about Bill Partridge;
Cheerful Sacrifice. The Battle of Arras 1917: Jonathan Nicholls. (Pen & Sword 1990)
Great War Portraits. Keith Collman: 2009

Note:
Bill Partridge was interviewed on tape by Jon Nicholls in February 1985 at his home at 97 Old House Road, Hemel Hempstead. Amongst the many things Bill spoke about was alcohol. He remembered how he hated French beer. 'Gnat's Piss' we called it!' but he loved Grenadine and had a fondness for Army Rum. 'It was good stuff.'

In September 1985, Bill Partridge made his last pilgrimage to the trenches with the Hampstead Pals.

Corporal Alfred 'Alf' Charles Razzell

8th (Service) Battalion, The Royal Fusiliers
Born 9 March 1897 – Died 20 January 1995 aged 97 years
To France & Flanders with the Hampstead Pals 1984 – 1991

LEFT. Alf Razzell 1916
RIGHT. Alf at Ovillers with the Hampstead Pals in 1985 *(Photo: Keith Collman)*

Roger Evans, Superintendent Metropolitan Police (Rtd) writes;

One of the unrepeatable privileges of visiting the old Western Front with a veteran soldier was the opportunity to hear - first hand, from one who was there - exactly what it was like to 'go over the top', a surely frightening experience.

Standing in a motley crowd of the Hampstead Pals on a French back road in 'Mash Valley' and listening to ex-Corporal Razzell relate, in calm and rational speech, the tale of the destruction of 8th Battalion, Royal Fusiliers on 7 July 1916, was an experience that I shall take to the grave. In fact, I have recounted this story to my son, standing in the same place some thirty years later. Before getting to this location, Alf had told us all the tale of the 8th Royal Fusiliers. He regaled us with affectionate stories of certain officers who remained firmly fixed in his memory some seventy years after the events of the Somme Offensive. The magnificently named, Colonel Albemarle Cator Annesley DSO was first in Alf's memory of those who led him and his companions into the teeth of Hell. Whilst Col. Annesley was hardly in his dotage at the age of 42, he must have seemed to be an 'old man' to the 17-year-old Alf Razzell who joined up in 1914. However, Alf regarded Col. Annesley with great respect, particularly when he joined the battalion in the 5-mile runs that were undertaken during basic training and when in France. Colonel Annesley evidently believed that all of his men were his 'lads'. On route marches, these lads would sing songs that would have made many people blush, but, according to Alf, the Colonel, at the head of his marching battalion, would pirouette and wave his cane (a lethal item without which no self-respecting officer would face the foe) and cry out, "Did you teach them this one, Bobby?" directed at his Adjutant, Captain Robertson-Walker.

Certain revisionist historians would have one believe that the British Army in the First World War were lions led by donkeys. Having had the honour to listen to Alf Razzell recount his experiences of life in the trenches, it is evident that he was led by men of the highest quality. Inter alia, Colonel Annesley, 'Bobby' Robertson-Walker, Robert Chard and Harry Featherstonehaugh were leaders worthy of their men.

The objective that the 8th Royal Fusiliers were assigned on 7 July 1916 should have been taken on the first day, 1 July. Whilst aware of the failure of the proceeding week, Alf's view was, "We were a good battalion". He had absolute faith that his mates and his officers would win the day. Alf Razzell was a Corporal on 7 July 1916. At the roll call at the end of that horrific day, Alf was the senior rank on parade.

The Hampstead Pals took Alf to visit Colonel Annesley who is buried in Warloy-Baillon cemetery. His headstone bears the lovely inscription;

'He greatly lived, he greatly loved and he died right mightily'

We must never forget such men.

Adapted from the Eulogy given by Jonathan Nicholls at the funeral of Alf Razzell on
7th February 1995

I first met Alf in March 1981 when he replied to a letter I had published in the
Watford Observer, asking for veteran soldiers of the Great War of 1914-18 to contact
me. Consequently, I was invited to his home at 38 Bradshaw Road, Watford. And it
was there, over tea and his wife Win's homemade cakes, that a lasting friendship was
forged. It was a happy meeting. Very memorable, for I remember vividly his
enthusiasm for my project but above all, his immense pride at having served with that
most famous of English Regiments, The Royal Fusiliers.

On this first visit, we drank tea. He wanted to offer me whisky but thought I was
on duty! But from then on, things changed. He was delighted to discover that I liked
whisky too. Even then, he made sure that I wasn't driving before he got the bottle out.
Whisky is great for unlocking the memory and, although his stories of the trenches
were chilling, we laughed heartily over his raucous 'barrack-room ballads' - tales of
active service in Kitchener's Army. What a marvellous sense of humour he possessed.
But above all, he was easy-going and loved conversation. He could relate to *anyone*,
especially young people. With Alf Razzell, there was no generation gap.

A native of South London, Alf was born in Lambeth on 9 March 1897 and was an electrical engineer by trade. Following the 1914-8 War, he married Win and moved to the northeast of England for several years. During that time, Beryl and Jim (they had two children) arrived and Alf loved to chat about those happy days when he and Win would set off for a picnic into the Yorkshire countryside on a motorbike, with little Beryl and Jim on board! Alf was also a very fit man. Despite the rigours of a German prisoner of war camp, he soon regained his strength and gained a reputation in the Durham area as a professional sprinter, in which capacity he would gamble on himself to win and usually did! In 1937, the family moved back down south and settled in Hertfordshire. He was a gifted man. Not only was he skilled at metalwork, but, following his retirement, he took up cabinet-making as a hobby. The beautiful furniture that adorns his home and the homes of his children is a testimony to his great skill. He was also a gifted artist and produced many lovely paintings.

Alf was an original Kitchener volunteer and at the age of 17, joined the Army in September 1914, serving on the Western Front as an infantryman with the 8th (Service) Battalion, The Royal Fusiliers. In 1915, he saw front-line action in the Ypres Salient and at the Battle of Loos and the Battle of the Craters in March 1916.

As Roger Evans has told us, on 7th July 1916, Alf Razzell - then a Corporal - went over the top with his battalion at the Battle of the Somme. In an ill-fated attack and attempt to capture the German fortified village of Ovillers, the 8th Battalion was practically annihilated by machine-gun fire, with every single officer falling casualty. The following day, Alf discovered that only one NCO - that was him - and 63 men had survived the carnage to answer roll call. A day later, he was ordered back onto the battlefield to collect the paybooks of his fallen comrades. A harrowing experience, the vivid memories of which never left him.

Just three weeks later, he was in action again during the Somme battle and was badly wounded at Pozieres when his jaw was broken by shrapnel. He was labelled 'walking wounded' and in spite of the loss of blood, made a painful journey on foot the two miles back to Albert and eventual evacuation to hospital in Blighty. It was in England, whilst recuperating from his wound, that he met the love of his life and wife-to-be, Win. Their happiness was not to last for long, however, because Alf was soon back on the Western Front in time for Sir Douglas Haig's next great push, the Battle of Arras, which opened on the 9th April 1917 and on that day, Alf's battalion played a successful role.

On 3rd May 1917, labelled by the official historian, Cyril Falls as 'The blackest day of the war', Alf shook hands with his chums and they went over the top together, advancing, in dawn's first light, over open country just east of Monchy Le Preux. Alf, with 25 of his mates, penetrated unscathed, deep into the enemy lines but their amazing luck ran out when they found themselves surrounded and heavily outnumbered by the enemy. The young Fusiliers knelt back-to-back and bravely fought to the last bullet. Soon, it was all over. All but two had perished.

Alf had tried to shoot his way out, accounting for many in the process, but he feigned death as the enemy overran them, lying among the bodies of his comrades for 24 hours. Eventually, German soldiers, searching the bodies for souvenirs and cigarettes, came to Alf who stood up and raised his hands. It was a desperate moment. Fortunately, he found himself face to face with a good man who did not kill him but took him prisoner.

Taken to the German trench, Alf found the badly wounded Bill Hubbard, one of pals with whom he had joined up back in August 1914. The Germans were leaving this part of the line in a hurry and Alf, in his determination to save his mate, tried to carry him, but the pain for Bill was too great. Reluctantly, Alf had to leave Bill in a shell hole, in the desolation that was the Arras battlefield.

Alf finally laid Bill's ghost to rest on 3 May 1984 at the age of 87, when he returned to the green fields of Monchy. On a grassy bank, he left a simple poppy wreath. 'In memory of my Pal, Bill Hubbard.' This pilgrimage was the first of many visits with Alf Razzell to the battlefields of France and the start of a long and happy association with the lads of Hampstead Police Station - The Hampstead Pals. He said it put an extra 10 years onto his life.

Alf was truly a star. In the nineties, he appeared in several television documentaries; *Lions Led by Donkeys, A Game of Ghosts,* and *The Nineties.* He also was the great inspiration behind *Cheerful Sacrifice,* eagerly reading each rough chapter as it was written. In 1993, he rose to fame in the music charts when he featured on lead vocals on the opening track, *The Ballad of Bill Hubbard* by Roger Waters of Pink Floyd, on an Album called *Amused to Death.*

In 1993 at the age of 96, he made 36 exhausting appearances in the London Theatre Production of *Voices of the Fallen,* a play (conceived and written by JN) about the poetry of the Great War. Alf was the star attraction, much to the annoyance of one of the actors, who was slightly jealous of Alf's popularity.

When the play was showing at Pentameters Theatre in Hampstead, for once, we had a full house and the lights went down for the start of the performance. Onto the stage walked our actor humming a First World War song as per script. Several attempts to strike the match to light up the dugout failed and our actor was getting visibly agitated. From the front row of the stalls came Alf's distinctly loud whisper, 'The cat's pissed on the matches!' which totally destroyed the solemnity of the moment and caused much laughter among the audience.

Alf and I spent a lot of time speaking to local schools which I know he loved doing. Our double act was more popular than Morecambe and Wise! Hundreds of London & Hertfordshire schoolchildren were held enthralled by his tales from the trenches.

Alf Razzell died at 97 on 20 January 1995. Prior to his death, we had spent a lot of time together and he had related & recorded further 'Tales from the Trenches' (not for the faint-hearted); hopefully, the full story, unexpurgated, will be told soon.

Alf Razzell looking pensive at the Lochnagar Mine Crater in 1984
Hampstead Police officers Peter Dumville (L) Steve Gilbert (Centre) and Michael
Curtis (R); in the background Cyril Nicholls.

Letter from Alf Razzell to the Hampstead Pals dated 20th May 1984

Dear Hampstead Pals,

Since I arrived home on Thursday last, I've spent the time re-living the journeys and excursions of our last five days in France. I was glad to be able to pay tribute to all my old comrades, especially Bill Hubbard and my old Colonel and, having done so, it gave me a feeling of contentment and peace.

I realise how much hard work and research had been done in locating the places of particular interest to me, such as the sunken road in front of Monchy-le-Preux, Mash Valley, Ovillers, etc. re-awakening sad but vivid memories after all these years.

Being with you, all the laughter, leg-pulling, jokes and songs reminded me of the comradeship of those days so long ago. I enjoyed the bus journeys, the picnics and especially the company of you all, not forgetting our time spent in the bar. I thought the last-night banquet was stupendous – I'm still enjoying that mentally.

It was all a unique experience and due to your kindness and generosity, a very happy one for me, which will remain with me for the rest of time.

Thank you all for making it possible.

Yours Sincerely

Alf

Ovillers 1916

A place of tortured sacrifice,
Like a rosary of tears and passion,
As young men's souls winged aloft
We grieve as Alf in humble fashion

The breeze plays gently on summer grass
As birdsong cleaves the air at night,
And through the years his enduring tears
Through mourning days and soulful nights

Now Pals in time renew Alf's vow,
A remembrance vow that we must keep,
So Alf can now rest in eternity,
Of ever-celestial sleep

Tony Spagnoly

Further Reading about Alf Razzell;
Cheerful Sacrifice; The Battle of Arras 1917: Jonathan Nicholls. (Pen & Sword 1990)
Great War Portraits: Keith Collman 2009

Note:
Alf returned to the battlefields with the Hampstead Pals five times from 1984 to 1991. On his last visit to Ovillers in 1991, he asked, 'Who will remember my battalion after I am gone?' He was assured that the Hampstead Pals would continue to visit that sacred place as long as life permits.

In 2016, the Hampstead Pals held a special ceremony at Ovillers Military Cemetery, one hundred years after the attack on the village. An engraved granite plaque was placed on the Duhallow Memorial, commemorating 35 missing Royal Fusiliers. The plaque is in memory of Alf Razzell and the 8th Battalion The Royal Fusiliers.

It is still there.

Private Charles Victor TAYLOR

7th (South Irish Horse) Battalion, The Royal Irish
Born 18 October 1896 – Died 25 January 1988 aged 92 years
To France & Flanders with the Hampstead Pals 1980 – 1983

LEFT. 'South Irish Horse. A Dubliner resting on his way to the Arras Front'
A charcoal sketch by (Sir) William Orpen. *Courtesy of the Imperial War Museum.*
RIGHT. Charlie Taylor on the Somme Battlefield at Hawthorne Ridge 1982 (Jon Nicholls)

Adapted from the Eulogy given by Jonathan Nicholls at the funeral of Charlie Taylor
on 3rd February 1988

I first met Charlie Taylor at his home at 20 Birchington Road, NW6 in January 1980
and it was there, in the company of his wife Lil and the temporary presence of freshly
made buttered scones and Bells Whisky, that a firm friendship was forged. Many

subsequent visits led me to find out much more about this charming old Irish gentleman.

Charlie was born on 18th October 1896, in Carlow, Southern Ireland. He attended the famous Christian Brothers School, and, in October 1914, he joined the British Army and became a trooper in a Cavalry Regiment, The South Irish Horse. Then, because he was still 18, he was accepted on condition that he sold his new bike to the recruiting sergeant!

At this time, Britain was suffering the agony of a second year of war with Germany, but for many impressionable young men like Charlie Taylor, who was indeed a true British patriot and Royalist, there was a great deal of adventure to be had. He would also be doing one thing that he loved - horse riding.

In the July of 1916, Charlie found himself among the squalor and horror of the Battle of the Somme, not riding a horse as he had hoped, in a glorious cavalry charge, but burying the dead in the trenches where they had fallen. One of the young soldiers Charlie laid to rest was his own cousin, Willie Taylor, killed near Guillemont in August 1916.

The following spring, Charlie was indeed in the saddle eagerly awaiting the opportunity of the breakthrough at the Battle of Arras. That breakthrough never came and the war dragged on through the summer of 1917 and into November when Charlie, at the Battle of Cambrai, to his dismay, found himself dismounted and in the infantry, which was the 7th (South Irish Horse) Battalion the Royal Irish. Somebody in high command at long last had realised that the usefulness of Cavalry in modern warfare was at an end.

The 21st of March 1918 was what Charlie described as 'the most dangerous day of his life' and it was on this day, at Bony, Nr St Quentin, that he was captured and made a prisoner of war. This was during the last great German offensive battle known as the 'Kaiser's Battle' that they hoped would win the war for them. Charlie was destined, along with thousands of other British soldiers, to suffer the rest of the war in the harsh confines of a prisoner of war camp. At the end of the war, Charlie weighed just seven stone and was thankful to be alive. He was also eternally thankful that the German soldiers who made him prisoner were Saxons. Many British soldiers did not see captivity on that day.

In 1920, Charlie joined the Liverpool City Police where he happily served for 25 years, marrying and raising a family of three daughters. In 1945, after suffering the rigours of the Liverpool Blitz, he retired from the Police and did what many police officers did in retirement and took a pub. Not happy with that lifestyle, he purchased a small boarding house on the Isle of Man but in 1953, he finally arrived in London and went to work for the Ministry of Defence in Whitehall. By then, he was a widower and it was in London in 1955 that he met Lil and they enjoyed a happy marriage of 33 years.

Charlie mesmerised us with his stories of the war and he certainly made us laugh when 'drinking wine in France'. Advancing years did nothing to improve his hearing and we will never forget the reply he gave one sunny picnic lunchtime when asked if he would like another glass of wine, he replied in his rich Irish brogue, "Just a sloice!"

Bill Hay keeps a watchful eye on his Parker pen that he has lent to Charlie At Guillemont Road Cemetery

Note:

Charlie returned to the battlefields with the Hampstead Pals three times from 1980 to 1983. Each time, we made a pilgrimage to Guillemont Road Cemetery and the grave of his 19-year-old cousin, Willy Taylor, 7th Battalion King's Liverpool Regiment and a wreath was laid on his grave. Also buried in this cemetery, which lies in the heart of the Somme Battlefield, is Raymond Asquith, the eldest son of the British Prime Minister. Today, the Hampstead Pals still visit Willy Taylor's grave at Guillemont Road Cemetery.

CHAPTER 4

These Names will be Found Again

Go and search ye o'er the battlefields,
These names will be found again
Each one inscribed on a cross
To show how they played the game.
They died; a handful of a mighty host
Who gave their lives that you and I
Might live. They died like men in foreign lands,
In the Club they will never die

From the Clifton Rugby Football Club memorial which lost 45 players in the Great
War and quoted from
'A Social History of English Rugby' by Tony Collins. (With kind permission of
Routledge)

John Buoy writes:

In May 2015, the Hampstead Pals (many of whom had played the wonderful game of Rugby Football) conducted a memorable 'Rugby Tour' of the Great War Battlefields of France and Belgium, many of us wearing our old club colours, visiting and commemorating the graves and memorials to brave soldiers who happened to be Rugby Football Internationals before making the ultimate sacrifice, serving King and Country in the Great War. Needless to say, an appropriate 'toast' was drunk to each player at his graveside in accordance with the traditions of the Hampstead Pals.

Rugby players were the first sportsmen to volunteer to join the forces in France and Belgium and International players were no exception, with over 130 British and Commonwealth players giving their lives, including 23 French players.

"Every player who represented England in International matches last year
has joined the colours"
The Times 30 November 1915.

Altogether, we visited the graves of 14 players from England, Wales, Ireland, Scotland and New Zealand who served in the war, giving up their lives at home, often leaving family members and halting their promising rugby careers to fight for our freedom, of which ten are commemorated in this book. Having served their country on the rugby fields, they were now prepared to serve their country on the battlefields! Unfortunately, some other sports, especially football, were not so quick to follow the lead of their rugby counterparts, hence the poster displayed below:

We placed mini rugby balls on each grave and memorial as a mark of respect for their efforts and to recognise their rugby talents, to show we will always remember them.

One very special player, David Gallaher (above) originally from Ireland, who emigrated to New Zealand, not only served in France in the Great War but had also served in Africa in the Boer War. Gallaher proceeded to become a legend in NZ rugby and is regarded as the father of rugby to this day. Famous English players like Edgar Mobbs and Jack Raphael at Lijssenthoek are also included in our list of visited heroes.

There are many more that we have not yet visited, but we will add them to future tours and give them the recognition they deserve.

Jon Buoy

Hampstead Pals

Harrow RFC. (1971 – 1974)

Saracens F.C. (1975 – 1995

Second Lieutenant Harry ALEXANDER

1st Battalion The Grenadier Guards. Aged 35
England Rugby Football International. 7 Caps.
Killed in action 17th October 1915. The Battle of Loos
Arras Road Cemetery, Roclincourt, France

John Buoy writes;

Harry Alexander was a professional singer when war broke out and was possessed of a beautiful baritone voice. Born in Birkenhead in Cheshire, his father, William, was a cotton broker in Liverpool and his mother, Edith, was the daughter of the little-known artist Robert Gathoney. Harry had one brother and two sisters.

He was educated firstly at Bromborough School, then Uppingham and on to Corpus Christie College, Oxford to study for a Classics degree. Between leaving

Oxford and the outbreak of war, he taught both privately and at Stanmore Prep School in London.

Whilst at Uppingham, he spent 2 years in the 1st XV, captained the school cricket XI and was a scratch golfer. At Oxford, he gained a double blue at Rugby in 1897 and 1898 and played for Cheshire, Birkenhead Park and Richmond Clubs. Soon, Harry was called up to represent England gaining 7 caps, and also played for the Barbarians. The harder the game the better he liked it and his shock head of auburn hair could always be seen close to the action. He wrote a book called *How to Play Rugby* in 1902 which was a coaching manual on the theory and practice of the game.

Harry was commissioned in the Grenadier Guards after volunteering in July 1915 and, after brief training at Sandhurst, travelled to France in October 1915 to join the 1st Battalion. He was involved in one of the final actions in the Battle of Loos on 17 October 1915 at the infamous Hohenzollern redoubt.

In the space of three hours, the battalion suffered 400 casualties of which Harry was one. He was killed exactly 13 days after arriving at the front. He was married to Louise Risby in 1913 and had one daughter, Jean, who was born a year later. His body was located by the (Imperial) War Graves Commission on the Loos Battlefield in September 1927 and identified by 'Regimental buttons and one star on each shoulder strap.'

Jon Buoy (Saracens) & Steve Page (British Army) respectfully conduct the Commemoration presentation at the grave of Harry Alexander in the Arras Road Cemetery.

Editor's Note:

This cemetery, which stands on the 1917 Arras Battlefield, is probably the first the visitor sees when leaving the A26 Motorway at the Arras exit from Calais. However, it is no longer possible to stop directly outside, as the Commonwealth War Graves Commission have sensibly closed the front entrance with a hedge. To gain safe entrance to the cemetery requires driving another mile further on the Arras by-pass and exiting at the Roclincourt-Ecurie turn-off, then doubling back, taking the narrow lane which was formerly the main Arras-Lens Road. After driving along this road, which crosses the old 1915 -1917 'No Man's land' (once heavily cratered and where a profusion of rusty metal including live shells is still upturned by the plough), one arrives at the Arras Road Cemetery. The road is just wide enough for a coach and continues to Nine Elms Cemetery where one can turn around.

In 1926, the Arras Road Cemetery was enlarged to take bodies being found during the late 1920s and early 1930s. Captain Arthur Kilby VC was found on the Loos battlefield and reburied in Arras Road Cemetery, his name being taken off the Loos Memorial to the Missing. Most of the graves in Arras Road Cemetery are unknown. In the mid-1930s, even this cemetery was becoming full, so Canadian No. 2 Cemetery on Vimy Ridge was enlarged and became the new open cemetery, not only for the Arras area but even from the Somme area. During the early 1960s, Canadian No.2 was almost full and bodies still being found were taken to Terlincthun Cemetery near Boulogne.

The Commonwealth War Graves Commission says;
Roclincourt was just within the British lines before the Battles of Arras, 1917; the 51st (Highland) and 34th Divisions advanced from the village on the 9th of April, 1917, and the 1st Canadian Division attacked on their left, across the Lens road. Arras Road Cemetery was begun by the 2nd Canadian Infantry Brigade soon after the 9th of April, 1917, and until the Armistice, it contained only the graves (now at the back of the cemetery) of 71 officers and men of the 7th Canadian Infantry Battalion (British Columbia Regiment) who fell in April, May and June, 1917; but between 1926 and 1929, it was enlarged by the addition of 993 graves from a wide area, mainly North and East of Arras. There are now over 1000 First World War casualties of which 264 are identified.

Serjeant David GALLAHER
2nd Battalion Auckland Regiment. Aged 43
New Zealand Rugby Football International. 6 Caps.
Killed in action 4th October 1917. The Battle of
Passchendaele
Nine Elms British Cemetery, Poperinge, Belgium

John Buoy writes;

David Gallagher (later Gallaher) was born on 30th October 1873 at Ramelton, County
Donegal, Northern Ireland, the son of James Henry Gallagher, the 7th of 14 children.

In 1878, the Gallagher family left Ireland for New Zealand and changed their name to Gallaher.

Having left school at 13 after his mother's death from cancer in September 1887, David took on some responsibility with his elder siblings to bring up the family in Freemans Bay which is where he took up Rugby Football.

In 1901, Gallaher enlisted in the 10th New Zealand Rifles and took part in the Boer War remaining in Africa for 18 months. A natural leader, he was promoted to Squadron Sergeant Major and returned to Auckland in August 1902.

He represented Auckland 26 times between 1903 and 1906 and received his first NZ cap at the tender age of 30 years, playing for his country 36 times and named as tour captain for the 1905 tour to the British Isles. On this tour, they were first given the name the All Blacks. David played 26 matches during this tour and the team won 31 of the 32 matches and scored 830 points conceding just 36 points. The only loss was against Wales in a memorable match watched by thousands.

"Hard as nails, fast and full of dash, he bolted from the mark every time, played right up to the whistle and stopped for nothing big or small"; so read his front-page obituary in the New Zealand press. He was the first player to use a game plan and employ science and strategy in the team. His existence was a massive contribution to the foundation and ethos of New Zealand Rugby. He is regarded as the father of rugby in New Zealand and plays a massive part in their sporting history.

David Gallaher retired from playing rugby in 1906 and became a coach and selector and wrote a book, 'The Complete Player'. That year, he married Ellen Ivy May Francis and had a daughter, Nora. Although exempt from conscription due to his age, Gallaher enlisted on 25 July 1916 (taking 3 years off his real age). Two of his brothers had already been killed in France so he felt it was the honourable thing to do. He was, in fact, 41 years old and was promoted to Serjeant and later Company Sergeant Major because of his experience in the Boer War.

On 16 February 1917, he sailed with the 2nd Battalion Auckland Light Infantry Regiment to Devonport, Plymouth and on to France. At first, he was in action near Ypres then prepared for the Passchendaele offensive and the Battle of Broodseinde.

At 06.00 hrs on 4 October 1917, Gallaher led his men over the top for the last time in the New Zealand Division's attack on the Gravenstafel Spur. A piece of shrapnel smashed through his helmet and he was carried, dying, from the battleground. He died hours later at the Australian No 3 Casualty Clearing Station, just weeks short of his 44th birthday. Altogether, the action on that part of the battlefield (known as

Broodseinde) claimed 330 New Zealand lives. It is said that a Padre visiting that grim place – not much more than a tunnel attached to one of the trenches - asked the soldier in the next bed if he knew who Gallaher was; the soldier said that he didn't. He received the reply: "That is Dave Gallaher, Captain of the 1905 All Blacks." In fact, he was one of 13 All Blacks to be killed in the First World War.

Of the 9 brothers in the Gallaher family, 5 fought in the Great War. Douglas was wounded in action at Gallipoli on 4 May 1915 and later died at Laventie, France on 3 June 1916.

David Gallaher died in action on 4 October 1917 and Henry was killed in action on 24 April 1918. Henry's twin brother, Charles, was shot in the back in Gallipoli and survived several years with a bullet lodged close to his spine. Laurence survived the war without any recorded injury. David Gallaher is buried at Nine Elms Cemetery in Poperinge, Belgium, not far from The Island of Ireland Peace Park in Messines. His grave bears the Silver Fern, the New Zealand emblem so proudly worn on the All Blacks' team shirt and has become a place of pilgrimage for All Blacks teams touring France.

Back in New Zealand, Gallaher is remembered with a 2.7-metres-high bronze statue outside Eden Park Stadium and Auckland clubs play for the Gallaher Shield each season. Each test match between France and New Zealand is contested for the Dave Gallaher Cup. In Donegal, Ireland, Gallaher's home town, a park has been built and named Dave Gallaher Park. The touring All Blacks visited the Park in 2005 whilst on tour. Several former All Black captains, such as Richie McCaw, Tana Umaga and Sean Fitzpatrick, have all paid tribute to their valiant predecessor over the years. Most of them have also either visited his grave or his birthplace in Ireland.

The famous New Zealand journalist and writer on rugby Sir Terry McLean said: "In death, he acquired a mystique. His grave became a shrine."

L-R Jon Buoy (Saracens) Peter Crew (Rosslyn Park) & John Amos (Met Police) conduct the Commemoration presentation at the grave of David Gallaher, standing on the sacred ground where successive All Black teams have stood.

The Commonwealth War Graves Commission says;

The cemetery was begun and used by the 3rd Australian and 44th Casualty Clearing Stations when they moved to Poperinghe (now Poperinge), from Brandhoek and Lijssenthoek respectively, in September 1917. Nearly all the burials in Plots I to IX came from these Casualty Clearing Stations whilst they operated in this area during the 1917 Battle of Ypres up until December 1917. Plots X, XI, XIII, XIV and XV cover the dates between the beginning of March 1918 and the 12th of October, 1918, the period of the German offensive in Flanders, the British counter-attacks and the final advance of August-September. The burials in these cases were carried out almost entirely by fighting units. The cemetery contains 1,556 Commonwealth burials of the First World War and 37 German war graves from this period. There are also 22 Second World War burials in the cemetery, all dating from the Allied retreat to Dunkirk in 1940. The cemetery was designed by Sir Reginald Blomfield.

Second Lieutenant Douglas (Danny) LAMBERT

6th Battalion The Buffs (East Kent Regiment) Aged 32
England Rugby Football International. 7 Caps.
Killed in action 13th October 1915. The Battle of Loos
The Loos Memorial, France.

John Buoy writes;

Douglas Lambert was born in Cranbrook on 14 October 1883 and educated at St Edward's in Oxford and later at Eastbourne College.

A big man who was both strong and fast which suited his chosen sport of Rugby Football. Known as 'Danny', he joined Harlequins club and played on the wing and was also a very good goal kicker. He was soon spotted by the England selection committee and played his first International against France on 5 January 1907 at Richmond. Lambert was outstanding and scored 5 tries in a very one-sided match, winning by 30 points. However, he was dropped for the rest of that season and played his next game in the following season against France and also played for Harlequins in the first match at the new stadium in Twickenham. On 28 January 1911, Lambert played for England against France and scored two tries, five conversions and two penalties, a grand total of 22 points. This was to remain a record number of points for an individual player until 1990. Danny was an all-round sportsman: he was also a scratch golfer, played football (soccer) for Corinthian Casuals, and kept wicket (cricket) for Hertfordshire.

With war being declared in August 1914, Lambert was commissioned as a 2nd Lieutenant in the 6th Battalion of the Royal East Kent Regiment (the Buffs). After marrying his childhood sweetheart, Joyce, at West Brompton on December 17 1914, he eventually travelled to France with his unit, leaving Joyce pregnant. The 6th Buffs were destined to take part in the Battle of Loos, a major offensive commencing on 25 September 1915. In this battle, gas was used for the first time by the British forces, with varying success.

On 13 October, after much fighting, with land being gained then lost to the Germans, the British tried one last effort to break through with the Buffs going over the top, led by their officers, to be met by a barrage of machine-gun fire from an unknown German trench. The battalion lost 400 men in just a few minutes, advancing just 100 yards. Danny Lambert was one of the dead along with 9 of his fellow officers. His body was never found and, therefore, has no known grave, but is commemorated on the Loos Memorial. Part of the memorial wall containing the names of over 20,000 missing men is shown in the photograph above.

His son was born just two months after his death.

For more information on the Loos memorial, see Chapter Two under 'Private Arthur Searle'

England V France 1911. Will be forever remembered as 'Lambert's Match on account of his scoring 22 points in the 37-0 victory.
Back Row.   FM Stoop, WE Mann, CH Pillman, AD Roberts, L Haigh, Mr EA Johns
Middle.   NA Wodehouse, D Lambert, AD Stoop, JGG Birkett (captain) R Dibble, LG Brown, AL Kewney
Front   JA King, ALH Gotley, SH Williams

The windswept open Loos Battlefield from The Loos Memorial at Dud Corner

Lieutenant Colonel Edgar MOBBS

7th Battalion Northamptonshire Regiment. Aged 35
England Rugby Football International. 7 Caps.
Killed in action 31st July 1917. The Battle of Passchendaele
The Menin Gate Memorial, Belgium

John Buoy writes;

Edgar Roberts Mobbs was born in Northampton on 29 June 1882, the son of Oliver and Elizabeth Mobbs and had 5 siblings. Oliver was a car salesman and Edgar followed in the profession after finishing his education at Bedford Modern School. He was a keen sportsman and played in the rugby, cricket and hockey teams.

After turning out for Olney, Weston Turks and Northampton Heathens, he decided to step up a level and joined the Northampton Saints, becoming captain from 1907 to 1913. He was a three quarter and scored a massive 177 tries during this period. A large, strong man, Mobbs played mostly on the wing as he was also a very good sprinter with a good hand-off and an exciting runner with the ball. He soon progressed to the East Midlands representative team and took on the touring Australians in December 1908, defeating them in Leicester, this being their only defeat on the tour.

In 1909, Mobbs faced Australia again, but this time in an England shirt and he scored the only England try, however, Australia won by 9 points to 3. He earned 7 caps for England in total, captaining the side on a few occasions. He was not selected after 1910 but continued to play for Northampton and the Barbarians and finally retired from rugby aged 31 years in 1913.

At the outbreak of war, he tried to enlist but was told he was too old so he enlisted as a private soldier and raised his own company of 250 like-minded sportsmen who became known as 'Mobbs' Own' and went on to form the backbone of the 7th Battalion Northamptonshire Regiment. Of the 250 who joined up, only 80 would survive the war.

In September 1915, Mobbs was posted to France and subsequently wounded at the Battle of Loos. He took command of the 7th Battalion after promotion to Major, then, a little later, to Lieutenant Colonel, during which time he was wounded on three occasions and Mentioned in Dispatches twice. In January 1917, Mobbs was awarded the DSO (Distinguished Service Order) and later that year was wounded again at Messines in June 1917. After 3 weeks' recovery, he was back with his battalion but unfortunately, during the Battle of Passchendaele, he was leading an attack from the front, despite his rank and was hit by enemy fire.

He was, apparently, attacking a machine-gun post, singlehandedly at some forlorn place called Lower Star Post near Zillebeke, when killed on 31 July 1917. Despite being shot through the neck and bleeding to death, he still had time to write out the position of the post to hand to a runner. His body was not recovered so he has no known grave and he is commemorated on the Menin Gate in Ypres, Belgium.

In his memory, a memorial match was played between the East Midlands XV and the Barbarians at Franklins Gardens, the home of Northampton RFC, a match that is still played to this day.

Nigel Stevens of the Commonwealth War Graves Commission explains the Commission's policy of commemorating the Missing of the Great War

Captain Thomas 'Tommy' Arthur NELSON

Lothians & Border Horse attached Machine Gun Corps.
Aged 40
Scotland Rugby Football International. 1 Cap.
Killed in action 9th April 1917. The Battle of Arras
Faubourg d'Amiens Cemetery, Arras, France

Jon Nicholls & John Buoy commemorate Tommy Nelson at Faubourg d'Amiens Cemetery, Arras

John Buoy writes;

Tommy Nelson was born on 22 September 1876, the son of the publisher Thomas Nelson and his wife Jessie Kemp. The family lived in Abden House in the south of

219

Edinburgh. Nelson obtained an estate at Achnacloich, on the shore of Loch Etive near Oban. He spent a considerable part of each year there.

He was educated at Edinburgh Academy, where he became a rugby union player. He played for a combined Edinburgh Academy - Watsons College schoolboy side in January 1895. He then went to study Classics at Oxford University, where he became a close friend of the writer, John Buchan. Nelson played rugby union for Oxford University, representing them from 1896. He captained the side in 1900. He was named in the Anglo-Scots side to face South of Scotland District on 25 December 1897; however, the match was called off!

He was originally named in the Provinces District side in December 1898, but his selection fell through. It was remarked that Nelson was not expected to turn out for the Provinces District in their match against Cities District on 14 January 1899. He was capped for Scotland in 1898. He rivalled Allan Smith for a place at centre three quarter, in the international side. It was thought that Nelson would get the nod in front of Smith for the Ireland match as Smith was struggling for fitness. Smith started that match but Nelson finally played alongside Smith at centre for the match against England.

In 1903, he married Margaret Balfour, the daughter of the Liverpool merchant, Alexander Balfour. They had six children, including Alexander Ronan Nelson (1906–1997) and Elisabeth Nelson (1912–1999) who married Lord Bryan Walter Guinness, then becoming Lady Moyne, Elizabeth Guinness.

Following his death, his widow Margaret married the famous French soldier, artist and writer Paul Maze (1887–1979). His book, *A Frenchman in Khaki* (1934), detailed his experiences of the action he saw on the Western Front. Winston Churchill wrote the foreword to his book.

While we are on the subject of books, The John Buchan novel *The Thirty-Nine Steps* (1915) is dedicated to Tommy who eventually became head of the family publishing firm of Thomas Nelson and Sons, which employed Buchan as literary advisor and was one of the writer's publishers.

He was renowned as a benevolent owner of the company. The publishing house had an athletics club and Nelson gave over a portion of his family estate so that the club could use it. The company was noted as a pioneer in looking after the health of its employees at the time by employing an official to look after their health.

During the Great War, Nelson became a Captain with the Lothians and Border Horse attached to the Machine Gun Corps. He then moved to special service with Tanks and was killed by a stray shell while on observation duty near Arras Railway

Station on the first day of the battle, 9 April 1917. He had been at the front for 18 months.

Ironically, his friend John Buchan's youngest brother, Alistair, was killed, aged 22, on the same day, while serving with the Royal Scots Fusiliers and is buried at Duisans Cemetery, Etrun. The Hampstead Pals have visited his grave on several occasions.

Tommy Nelson is buried in Faubourg d'Amiens Cemetery, Arras. He is also memorialised on his parents' grave in Grange Cemetery in south Edinburgh.

He was quite a wealthy man and The Hull Daily Mail headlined 'A Publisher's Fortune', detailing that Nelson of Achnacloich in Argyll left an estate of £470,782, of which £219,300 represented his holding in the publishing firm.

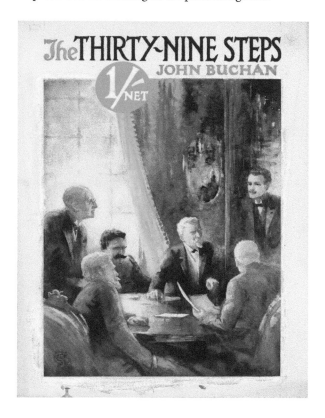

TO

THOMAS ARTHUR NELSON

(LOTHIANS AND BORDER HORSE)

My dear Tommy, You and I have long cherished an affection for that elemental type of tale which Americans call the "dime novel" and which we know as the "shocker"— the romance where the incidents defy the probabilities, and march just inside the borders of the possible. During an illness last winter, I exhausted my store of those aids to cheerfulness, and was driven to write one for myself. This little volume is the result, and I should like to put your name on it in memory of our long friendship, in the days when the wildest fictions are so much less improbable than the facts.

John Buchan. Sept 1915.

Private James 'Peary' PEARSON

9th Battalion The Royal Scots. Aged 26
Scotland Rugby Football International. 12 Caps.
Killed in action 22 May 1915. The 2nd Battle of Ypres
Sanctuary Wood Cemetery, France

Bill Gemmell reads a tribute to Jimmy Pearson at Sanctuary Wood.
Nearby is Bill Hay's resting place.

John Buoy writes;

Private James Pearson was born on 24 February 1889 as the second son of William
Pearson, a stone mason and Isabella from Dalkeith in Scotland. He had brothers,
William and Robert and a sister, Mary. He attended George Watson's College from
1896 and soon became an excellent cricketer then later took up rugby football.

Pearson was an excellent athlete, and, on leaving school, he joined Watsonians, the old boys' club to his school, where he excelled in rugby, cricket and athletics. He was an excellent batsman and set a record within the club for the best batting average for 52 years. He was very slight and this held back his rugby career although he was very tenacious and extremely quick. Pearson scored an amazing 103 tries for Watsonians between 1909 and 1914, winning the championship four times.

He went on to represent Scotland on 12 occasions and overcame his lack of physical presence with real 'jinking' talent, scoring several tries. He intermingled his skill at rugby with several other sports including tennis, badminton, golf and soccer.

At the outbreak of war, he enlisted into the ranks of the 9th Battalion, The Royal Scots, becoming Private 2061 Pearson. He left for the front on his 26th birthday, 24 February 1915.

Late in the afternoon on 22 May 1915, word came down the trenches and passed like wild fire that Pearson, the rugby international and the most notable of men still remaining in the ranks of the 9th, had been killed. During fighting in Sanctuary Wood in Ypres, James Pearson was killed by a sniper while going along the trenches fetching water for himself and his comrades.

He is buried in Sanctuary Wood Cemetery, Ieper, Belgium and is remembered in the archives of the Scotland RFU and Watsonians Club.

An Old Comrade in the Royal Scots said in 1930,
'Sanctuary Wood has many memories, but there is one which transcends all others – the sight of the wee white face with the little smile as we filed past the little athlete lying in his last long sleep, clad not in the panoply of greatness, which he deserved, but in the common tunic and kilt of a private lying like a warrior taking his rest…. His name was known and loved by thousands. Countless times he had thrilled them with his genius, and now, in the sacred cause, he had laid down his life as a humble soldier. Never again will the little round-shouldered figure, with its long arms and gloved hands, gather a ball unerringly as of yore; but there must always be one spot in Sanctuary Wood that is for ever hallowed in Scottish rugger hearts – the resting place of Jimmy P, peerless three-quarter, private soldier and gentleman'.

Bill Hay remembered,
'We had several notable sportsmen in my company including a couple of Manchester City footballers, the Broad brothers. But without doubt the most famous of our

sportsmen to be killed was Jimmy Pearson, who was a famous Scottish Rugby International, a good pal and a lovely character. It was a terrible shock when we found out he had been killed. We vowed revenge on the bloody Germans who had caused so much sorrow. He lies in the same row of graves as some of my mates in the Dandy Ninth, including my great pal, Jocky Jack.'

Editor's Note:

Bill Hay's ashes were placed, at his request, on the grave of 'Jocky Jack' by the Hampstead Pals in March 1985. (See Chapter three)

Lieutenant Jack RAPHAEL
18th Battalion The King's Royal Rifle Corps. Aged 35
England Rugby Football International. 9 Caps.
Killed in action 11th June 1917. The Battle of Messines Ridge.
Lijssenthoek Military Cemetery, Belgium.

John Buoy writes;

By kind permission of the *Daily Express* newspaper, we have reproduced the beautifully written article by Lesley Bellew published on 27 March 2014.

'Mother reunited at last with her First World War hero son'

A fine sportsman and talented barrister, Jack Raphael died in a Flanders field in the First World War. His bereft mother's dying wish was to be reunited with her son, but how she managed it has remained a secret until now. Here, we exclusively reveal their tragic tale.

On a chilly autumn afternoon in 1929, a chauffeur-driven car pulled into the Lijssenthoek military cemetery in Flanders. Head groundsman, Walter Sutherland initially paid little attention as a finely dressed woman stepped out. More than a decade after the Great War, such pilgrimages by grief-stricken widows and mothers were common.

Sutherland glanced up ready to direct the visitor to one of the 11,000 identical stone graves. Once there, she would, like most who had preceded her, weep and lay flowers. However, there was something about the woman's purposeful stride and dry-eyed demeanour that alerted the worker that this was no ordinary mourner.

Introducing herself as Harriette Raphael, the woman outlined her extraordinary proposal. She explained that she was the mother of Lieutenant John Raphael who had been killed at the Battle of Messines Ridge in Belgium in June 1917 and buried at Lijssenthoek.

Now in poor health, her one remaining wish was to be laid to rest alongside her beloved only son. Mrs Raphael knew very well that military rules of the period strictly forbade such requests, explaining her decision to go directly to the gardener rather than making an official approach to the Imperial War Graves Commission.

The widow of multi-millionaire financier Albert Raphael, who was part of a banking dynasty that in the 1920s rivalled the Rothschild family, she was no doubt used to getting her way. A kindly man, Sutherland was also sympathetic to the plight of a generation of mothers who had suffered the tragedy of outliving their sons. Originally from Inverness, he too had fought in the war before marrying a Flanders girl and settling in Belgium.

Mystery surrounds the exact nature of the pact she made with Walter but 13 months later, a package arrived at the cemetery. It contained her ashes and the gardener knew precisely what he must do.

Without telling a soul, he sought out the fallen soldier's tombstone and, beside it, dug a small hole. Within a few minutes, the ashes were buried and the turf replaced.

Sutherland must have known he was taking a risk which could have cost him his job but within a few weeks, the signs of the burial were gone. The secret has remained in the workman's family for more than 80 years but now Sutherland's son George has decided to make public the story of a grieving mother's devotion.

George, 92, who was passed the secret by his father, says: "My father was moved by her determination. He showed me where he had cut out an area of grass and slipped the urn underneath. What he did was in defiance of the rules so he knew that he could not mark her name on the grave but he said a short prayer and always said he had 'done right'."

Although Walter and his family had no connection to the Raphaels, they became fascinated by the dead soldier. They set about researching his background and discovered that John Raphael, who was known as Jack, was a remarkable man cut down in his prime. It was understandable that his loss cast a shadow over the remainder of his mother's life.

Jack was born in Brussels in 1882 although his parents came from Hendon and moved back to London to start his education. He attended Merchant Taylors' School and went on to St John's College Oxford where he excelled at rugby, cricket and water polo.

The brilliant all-round sportsman led the British Lions' tour to Argentina in 1910, he won nine caps playing for England, getting his picture on a cigarette playing card and played cricket for Surrey.

Jack chose a career in law, becoming a member of Lincoln's Inn and was called to the Bar in 1908. He also took a great interest in politics and stood, albeit unsuccessfully, as the Liberal candidate for Croydon.

At the outbreak of war, his dream to enter Parliament and follow in the footsteps of his cousin Sir Herbert Raphael, MP for West Derby, was placed on hold.

From August 1914, he served as an officer with the Duke of Wellington's (West Riding) Regiment and later joined the 18th Battalion King's Royal Rifle Corps.

His exploits on the battlefield mirrored those on the sports arena but his luck ran out when he was hit by a German shell at St Eloi, 10 miles south of Ypres, early in the summer of 1917.

Harriette received a telegram on June 7 relaying the dreaded news that Jack had been injured. She was already grieving for her husband Albert who had died aged 73 while Jack was away at war.

All she could do was hope for Jack's recovery but within days, a second telegram confirmed her son's death on June 11 aged 35. To the end, Jack showed great courage, and, while gravely injured, learned the allies' attack had brought about the capture of Messines Ridge.

To mark his extraordinary valour, a fellow officer who was with him when he was wounded wrote: "I have seen gallant men in many parts of the world but never have I been so impressed by such a magnificent display of sheer pluck and unselfishness as was shown by Lieutenant JE Raphael."

Obituaries highlighted his sporting prowess: "A beautiful kick, a brilliant fielder and possessed of a good turn of speed, he was a fine natural player. On the cricket field and still more in the world of rugby football, a distinct personality. Everything he did created more than ordinary interest, his popularity as a man, apart from his ability, counting for much."

No amount of condolences could ease Harriette's pain. She was bereft and threw herself into immortalising her beloved son's memory. Harriette organised a service at St Jude-on-the-Hill Church in Hampstead Garden Suburb near the family home in north London and commissioned sculptor Charles Sykes, designer of the Rolls-Royce mascot the Spirit of Ecstasy, to create a memorial to her son. The marble plaque with a bust of Jack under the evocative motto "If character be destiny then his is assured" was unveiled on the north wall of St Jude-on-the-Hill by John Nairn, headmaster of Merchant Taylors'.

Jack's book, '*Modern Rugby Football*' was all but completed before he went to war so Harriette oversaw the printing of the 296-page coaching manual. She also founded a scholarship in his name at Oxford University. His memorial's motto was included in the book's foreword and the same words were inscribed on his headstone at Lijssenthoek, the second-largest allied cemetery in Belgium.

Later in life, Harriette, who died aged 73, dabbled with Buddhism as she struggled to comprehend her son's death. Yet always in the background was her burning desire to be buried next to Jack.

George Sutherland, who also tended the grounds at Lijssenthoek, says: "For years, whenever I was planting or cutting grass near the grave, I would always think about Mrs Raphael who, like all those other mothers, never recovered from losing a son in the Great War.

"I swear that my father's actions allowed Harriette and her son to rest together in peace."

The rules banning family burials in military cemeteries were finally relaxed in the 1960s.

Jack Raphael's sporting life

Rugby: Jack Raphael won his first cap in 1902 when England took on Wales in the Home Nations Championship. A centre, winger or full-back, he also played in the 1905 and 1906 Championships as well as in Test matches against France and New Zealand. He captained the 1910 British Lions tour to Argentina, which included the South American nation's inaugural Test match. He also wrote the book, *Modern Rugby Football*, published after his death.

Cricket: A right-handed batsman, Raphael captained Surrey CCC and also played for Marylebone CC, Gentlemen of England, London County and an England XI. Four of his five centuries were scored for Oxford University, including his career-best score of 201, which he made against Yorkshire. It remains the only double century made by an Oxford cricketer against Yorkshire. His century for Surrey came in the 1904 County Championship, scoring 111 against Worcestershire.

The Commonwealth War Graves Commission says;

During the First World War, the village of Lijssenthoek was situated on the main communication line between the Allied military bases in the rear and the Ypres battlefields. Close to the Front, but out of the extreme range of most German field artillery, it became a natural place to establish casualty clearing stations. The cemetery was first used by the French 15th Hôpital D'Évacuation and in June 1915, it began to be used by casualty clearing stations of the Commonwealth forces.

From April to August 1918, the casualty clearing stations fell back before the German advance and field ambulances (including a French ambulance) took their places.

The cemetery contains 9,901 Commonwealth burials of the First World War, 24 being unidentified. There are 883 war graves of other nationalities, mostly French and German; 11 of these are unidentified. There is 1 Non-World War burial here.

Eight of the headstones are Special Memorials to men known to be buried in this cemetery; these are located together alongside Plot 32 near the Stone of Remembrance.

The cemetery, designed by Sir Reginald Blomfield, is the second-largest Commonwealth cemetery in Belgium.

Lieutenant Francis (Frank) Nathaniel TARR

4th Battalion The Leicestershire Regiment. Aged 28
England Rugby Football International. 4 Caps.
Killed in action 18th July 1915, Zillebeke Lake, Nr Ypres
Railway Dugouts Burial Ground, Ypres, Belgium

Leicester Tigers Rugby fan, Barbara Middleton (Detective Sergeant Metropolitan
Police Rtd) pays tribute to Frank Tarr at Railway Dugouts Burial Ground

John Buoy writes,

Francis Nathaniel Tarr, known as Frank, was born at Ironville, near Belper,
Derbyshire, the only son of Frederick and Emma Tarr. Francis had an elder sister,
Mabel.

He was educated firstly at Stoneygate School, Leicester and later Uppingham. Francis went to University College, Oxford (1906-1910) to read law and became a solicitor in Leicester. His rugby career started at school, playing for the Uppingham 1st XV for 2 years, then gaining a triple blue at Oxford, the last of these being the famous match where Ronnie Poulton Palmer scored 5 tries. Tarr, unfortunately, broke his collar bone during this match.

Three of Tarr's four caps, playing at centre, came in the 1908-09 season, including the game against France where he scored two tries in front of his home crowd at Welford Road, Leicester. The fourth cap came four years later in a Calcutta Cup match as part of England's Grand Slam. Altogether, Frank made 94 appearances for the Leicester 1st team between 1906 and 1913, and scored 24 tries.

At Oxford, Tarr had been a Cadet Sergeant in the Officer Training Corps and had joined the 1/4th Battalion of the Leicestershire Regiment as a Territorial Second Lieutenant in 1911, gaining promotion to full Lieutenant in 1913. When war came, he enlisted immediately and went with the battalion to the Western Front in March 1915.

Four months later on the 18 July 1915, Tarr was visiting the Lake Zillebeke dugouts which were being heavily shelled by the Germans and after sticking his head out of the hole to warn some men to keep down, he was hit in the face by a splinter from an exploding shell. That night, surrounded by friends, he was buried not far from where he had fallen. It was a very sad service led by the Brigade Chaplain, Reverend Paul Ashby, as Tarr was immensely popular and regarded as a born leader in the regiment, a rugby international and the idol of the machine gun section. As darkness fell, Tarr was buried with silent salutes and stifled tears.

He is also remembered on the family headstone in Welford Road Cemetery, and on memorials at Leicester Rugby Club, Uppingham School, University College (Oxford), Oxford University RFC, the Richmond Athletic Ground (Richmond FC), and at the RFU Museum at Twickenham (where his name is among 27 on a Memorial Board to England Rugby Internationals who fell in the First World War).

Herewith is an extract from 'Footprints of the 1/4th Leicestershire Regiment' by Captain John Milne: Chapter IX - HILL 60

"From July 13th to the 19th, the battalion remained comfortably in the railway dugouts basking in the sunshine and complacently watching Ypres being shelled during the day and uncomplainingly carrying out fatigues by night. So far so good. On the 18th, however, there was a tragedy. Lieut. F. N. Tarr was killed. You had to know

Frank Tarr and to be in the battalion to realise what that meant; no words can ever explain.

He was killed by a splinter from a 'Krump' whilst he was visiting the Zillebeke Lake dugouts. The Bosche was industriously shelling a field cooker which stood under a hedge close by, and Tarr put his head out of a dugout to tell some men to keep under cover when a splinter hit him in the face. If it had been any other part of his body, it would have caused only the slightest of wounds, a mere scratch, but that only made it more tragic. This happened in the afternoon.

That night, surrounded by his friends, he was buried not very far from where he had fallen, and the Brigade Chaplain (Rev. Paul Ashby) read the burial service. It was a sad night for everybody, for Frank Tarr was the most attractive personality in the battalion; young, good-looking, full of charm, with an eye that always had a twinkle in it, a born leader, yet the kindest person possible, a rugger international and the idol of the machine-gun section, which he commanded before he became adjutant.

Everybody was heartbroken, for everybody would miss him; they would not look upon his like again. And so, as the darkness fell, they buried him by stealth, with silent salutes and stifled tears. And the transport officer (Lt W.B. Jarvis), who had played David to his Jonathan, caused a large white cross of wood to be made, a larger cross than any which stood around, that all who passed might see and remember a great three-quarter and a greater gentleman.'

A memorial service to commemorate the life of Frank Tarr was held at Leicester FC's home ground at Welford Road on 10 May 2009; The Last Post was sounded simultaneously in Leicester and at Ypres.

The Commonwealth War Graves Commission says;

Railway Dugouts Cemetery is 2 kms west of Zillebeke village, where the railway runs on an embankment overlooking a small farmstead, which was known to the troops as Transport Farm. The site of the cemetery was screened by slightly rising ground to the east, and burials began there in April 1915. They continued until the Armistice, especially in 1916 and 1917, when Advanced Dressing Stations were placed in the dugouts and the farm. They were made in small groups without any definite arrangement and in the summer of 1917, a considerable number were obliterated by shell fire before they could be marked. The names "Railway Dugouts" and "Transport Farm" were both used for the cemetery. At the time of the Armistice, more than 1,700 graves in the cemetery were known and marked. Other graves were then brought in from the battlefields and small cemeteries in the vicinity, and a number of the known graves destroyed by artillery fire were specially commemorated. The latter were mainly in the present Plots IV and VII.

The cemetery now contains 2,459 Commonwealth burials and commemorations of the First World War. 430 of the burials are unidentified and 261 casualties are represented by special memorials. Other special memorials record the names of 72 casualties buried in Valley Cottages and Transport Farm Annexe Cemeteries whose graves were destroyed in later fighting. The cemetery was designed by Sir Edwin Lutyens.

26.05.15
Railway
Dugouts
Cemetery

Captain Alexander Findlater TODD

1st Battalion The Norfolk Regiment. Aged 41
England Rugby Football International. 2 Caps.
Died of Wounds 21 April 1915. The Assault on Hill 60
Poperinghe Old Military Cemetery, Belgium

John Buoy writes;

Alexander Todd was born on 20 September 1873 in Forest Hill, London, the son of
Bruce Beveridge Todd, a wine merchant and Phoebe Brooker. Educated at Mill Hill
school, he was captain of the association soccer team, cricket XI and rugby XV as a
talented forward. He went to Cambridge University in 1892 gaining a triple blue in

rugby football. After university, he joined the family business and played for Blackheath, Kent and the Barbarians. (1894).

He was invited to join the 1896 British Isles (before they were the Lions) tour of South Africa. Aged 23 and a handsome man, he drew admiring comments from both the rugby writers of South Africa and from the ladies. Todd played in all four Tests against South Africa which ended in three wins for the tourists, and a loss in the final game played at Cape Town. In the Second Test, which the British team won by the largest margin, all three tries came from forward positions, one of them being scored by Todd; his first and only international points. He gained 2 caps for England which both came in 1900 whilst with the Blackheath club (he also played for Rosslyn Park), in the matches v Ireland and Scotland. England won the first of these 15-4 at Richmond, and then drew 0-0 in Edinburgh. He also played as wicket-keeper for Berkshire County at cricket.

During the Boer War in South Africa, Todd joined Robert's Horse and Carrington's Horse (squadron commander). During the campaign, he was wounded in action while fighting at Diamond Hill, and, on his return to Britain, he set up business in London and married Alice Mary Crean on 2 December 1902, the sister of Tom Crean who was a fellow tourist to South Africa. (Tom Crean also served in the Boer War and won a VC at the Battle of Tygerskloof). They had two children, Constance Mary (b.1905) and Bruce Edward (b.1908).

On September 21 1914, Todd was commissioned into the Norfolk Regiment at the outbreak of war. He was sent to France in October 1914 where he rose to the rank of Captain and was mentioned in Dispatches whilst serving with the 1st Battalion Norfolk Regiment at the infamous Hill 60. On April 18 1915, the day after he returned from leave, Todd was shot through the neck and died of his wounds on 21 April 1915. His men had previously expressed their concerns about his height whilst in the trenches as he was 6'2" tall; a sniper's ideal target.

Editor's Note:

A sad sequel…

In 1998, I purchased the rare book 'Rugby Football Internationals Roll of Honour' from a military book seller. When the book was delivered, I was intrigued to see that it had previously belonged to *Bruce Todd* of Arundel (Sussex), the only son of Alexander Findlater Todd. Written in pencil in the book was 'page 210 Daddy'.

I still have that book and refer to it often. I guess little son Bruce has long passed from this life but it still brings a tear to my eye.

The Commonwealth War Graves Commission says;

The town of Poperinghe (now Poperinge) was of great importance during the First World War because, although occasionally bombed or bombarded at long range, it was the nearest place to Ypres (now Ieper) which was both considerable in size and reasonably safe. It was, at first, a centre for Casualty Clearing Stations, but by 1916, it became necessary to move these units further back and field ambulances took their places.

The earliest Commonwealth graves in the town are in the communal cemetery, which was used from October 1914 to March 1915. The Old Military Cemetery was made in the course of the First Battle of Ypres and was closed, so far as Commonwealth burials are concerned, at the beginning of May 1915. The New Military Cemetery was established in June 1915.

The Old Military Cemetery contains 450 Commonwealth burials and commemorations of the First World War. 24 of the burials are unidentified but there are special memorials to seven casualties known or believed to be buried among them.

The graves of about 800 French and Belgian soldiers and nearly 500 civilians were removed from the cemetery after the Armistice. For the most part, the civilians died in an epidemic of typhoid at the end of 1914, and were buried from an emergency hospital housed in a neighbouring chateau.

The cemetery was designed by Sir Reginald Blomfield.

Second Lieutenant Phillip 'Phil' Dudley WALLER

71 Siege Battery South African Heavy Artillery. Aged 28
Wales Rugby Football International. 6 Caps.
Killed in action 14th December 1917
Red Cross Corner Cemetery, Beugny, France.

Ray Schofield-Almond and Jon Buoy relate the tragic story of Phil Waller and Percy Fitzpatrick and the introduction of the 2-minute silence on Armistice Day.

John Buoy writes;

Philip Dudley Waller was born on 28 January 1889 in Bath, Somerset. He was the son of Mr A P and Mrs E Waller from Alloa in Scotland. The family settled in Wales at

Carmarthen and Philip attended Carmarthen Intermediate School where he became a very keen athlete and sportsman. On leaving school in 1906, he was apprenticed as an engineer to the Alexander Dock Railway Company. He started to play rugby for Newport Rugby Football Club and was soon identified as a rising star by the Welsh Rugby Union. He was selected for Wales and played every match in the 1909 season, winning the Triple Crown. In 1910, he played against France and Australia and later that season, he went to South Africa with the British Isles team, (The 'Lions') playing in 23 of the 24 matches. He must have enjoyed the country so much as he decided to stay behind in South Africa when he was offered a job as an engineer for the Johannesburg Municipality. He settled in Johannesburg, even becoming a member of the town council there.

Phil enlisted as a gunner in the 71st (South African) Siege Battery which was raised in Transvaal. On arrival in England in February 1916, prior to going to France, Waller was stationed in Bexhill-on-Sea. He saw action on the Somme in 1916 and in the major battles of the following year. In May 1917, he was commissioned in the field and was later promoted to lieutenant but he did not survive very long after this.

A little over a week after the Battle of Cambrai, Lieutenant Waller was going home on leave. He and fellow rugby player and friend, Major Percy Fitzpatrick, had only just left their battery at Beaumetz-lès-Cambrai, when the shell struck killing them both instantly. He was buried at the small and intimate Red Cross Corner Cemetery at the nearby village of Beugny. *The Llanelli Star* wrote that he "had a wide circle of friends who regret his untimely though glorious death."

A few months later, the *Cambria Daily Leader* reported the death of his brother – "Richard Percy Waller, R.A.F., has been killed at Montrose. He had gained his wings as a pilot only a week before his death." (3 June 1918) The War memorial in their home town of Llanelli does not list the names of the servicemen commemorated there, but the names of both brothers can be found on the Carmarthen County War Memorial Roll.

Phil Waller was 28 years old and unmarried.

Red Cross Corner Cemetery.

New Welsh Caps

PHILIP DUDLEY WALLER, the Newport forward, who gets his first Welsh cap to-day, may be said to have experienced a phenominal rise to football fame. It was only in the season 1906 7 that he started playing

P. D. WALLER (Newport).

football for the Newport Third team. Last season he joined Newport Firsts. Born at Bath nineteen years ago, he has a qualification for Somerset, which county he has assisted on two occasions—at Cardiff against Glamorgan last season and at Taunton against the Wallabies a couple of weeks ago. He is an engineering apprentice at Alexandra Docks shops, under Mr. T. W. Pearson, the ex-Cardiff, Newport, and Welsh three-quarter.

Editor's note:

THE ORIGIN OF THE TWO-MINUTE SILENCE

While at Red Cross Corner Cemetery, *Ray Schofield-Almond* produced a fascinating story and told the Hampstead Pals that the practice of observing two minutes silence on Remembrance Sunday was initiated by the father of Major Percy Fitzpatrick, (Sir Percy Fitzpatrick) who lies in the next grave to Phil Waller. He suggested the idea of the two-minute silence, which had previously been carried out in South Africa, in a letter to King George V. The King was enthusiastic and sought approval from the War Cabinet on 5 November. It was immediately approved and a press statement was released from the Palace on 7 November 1919, which was immediately published in The Times:

To all my people,

Tuesday next, 11 November, is the first anniversary of the Armistice, which stayed the world-wide carnage of the four preceding years, and marked the victory of right and freedom.

I believe that my people in every part of the Empire fervently wish to perpetuate the memory of that great deliverance and of those who laid down their lives to achieve it.

To afford an opportunity for the universal expression of this feeling, it is my desire and hope that at the hour when the Armistice came into force, the 11th hour of the 11th day of the 11th month, there may be, for the brief space of two minutes, a complete suspension of all our normal activities.

During that time, except in the rare cases where this may be impracticable, all work, all sound, and all locomotion should cease, so that, in perfect stillness, the thoughts of everyone may be concentrated on reverent remembrance of the glorious dead.

No elaborate organisation appears to be necessary.

At a given signal, which could easily be arranged to suit the circumstances of each locality, I believe that we shall all gladly interrupt our business and pleasure, whatever it may be, and unite in this simple service of silence and remembrance.

GEORGE R.I

The Commonwealth War Graves Commission says of Red Cross Corner Cemetery;

Plot I of the cemetery (except Row K) was made between April 1917 and March 1918 by field ambulances and fighting units. When the cemetery fell into German hands in March 1918, they added the 25 Commonwealth burials that make up Row K (all from 21 March 1918) and began another cemetery alongside (Beugny Military Cemetery No.3). Commonwealth forces retook the cemetery in September 1918 and added Plot II to the original burials. The German graves were removed after the Armistice, and the Commonwealth burials among them were transferred partly to Delsaux Farm Cemetery and partly to Favreuil British Cemetery. Red Cross Corner Cemetery now contains 219 Commonwealth burials and commemorations of the First World War. 12 of the burials are unidentified and one casualty, whose grave was destroyed by shell fire in 1918, is commemorated by a special memorial. The cemetery was designed b y W H Cowlishaw.

CHAPTER 5

The Hares of the Somme

The Hares of the Somme

On Pal's trips we see them,
The Hares of the Somme,
At High Wood, another at Hamel
running pell mell on
ground where young men fell …

The Hares of the Somme

To Jack Rabbits they're akin,
born with eyes wide open,
and fully furred. They live in
forms, or folds in the ground.
Not warrens, below unseen:
as the Huns in nineteen sixteen;
who, on that first ghastly day
surfaced, and machine gunned
until fields ran with blood.

How did the Hares manage
to survive the Great War?
God knows what horrors
their ancestors saw.
With innate animal instinct
did they evacuate the ground
and quietly await events:
whilst armies fought around,
intent on killing each other.

Today, the Hares of the Somme
grow healthy and strong;
with boundless energy, and no fear,
they run, oblivious
of what once happened here.

Eric Page. Principal Surveyor, Metropolitan Police.

Pals: In the photo is veteran soldiers Alf Razzell & Bill Partridge *Photo: Keith Collman*
(with the proprietors of Le Relais Fleuri Albert, Michel & Nadia Fardel)

Pals: Verdun Police Station 1985.
Commander Jon Nicholls meets Commander Paul Nicolas
In the photo is veteran soldier Alf Razzell

Pals: Jon Nicholls, Sir John Stevens QPM KStJ, John Grieve QPM. CBE

Pals: Nick Batt

Photo: Sue Brown

The Old Vitasse Road 1918 (by unknown German Soldier)

The Old Vitasse Road 2008

Fragments of Remembrance…

The poppy bends and sways so gently
As in flight the winged dove
And at the close of golden evening
Bids you sleep with a hymn of love.

So, sleep on valiant warrior
In that beauteous land we cannot see
A place where tender hands of loved ones
Will watch, love and care for thee

Anthony Spagnoly
1928-2008

Acknowledgements

The inspiration for writing (or rather 'editing') this gentle project, 'Fragments of Remembrance', came after a telephone chat with John Grieve during the dismal Covid-19 'lockdown' in 2020. I consequently wrote via email to my Hampstead Pals, (mainly ex-Metropolitan Police) and an idea for the format of the book started to take shape in my head. There were several grandsons who had travelled with the Pals over the years and certainly some great-nephews and nieces. So why not offer them a lasting platform to tell the story of their missing loved one in the form of a book?

We considered that we had made many, *personal* visits to graves in France with a distinct family connection and this would create an embryo which would provide a lasting memory to these 'previously unknown' family sacrifices.

We did not wish to present any stories, war poetry or illustrations which have been presented before and often repeated in many books; the VC winners and rugby players excepted. We needed fresh literary material too. Step forward, Tim Savage, a retired police officer who generously contributed three of his unpublished poems. Likewise, Eric Page with his 'Hares of the Somme' and our dear departed friend, and companion to the battlefields, Anthony Spagnoly, who gave spiritual inspiration from 'The Other Side'. Those who were privileged to know him will understand.

Charles Pope VC was a unique case in so far as he was once a Metropolitan Police Officer at Chelsea Division, which drew immediate interest not only from his granddaughter and grandson, but also from the hierarchy of the Metropolitan Police, in the form of two Commissioners, one serving and one to be, who, on separate occasions, joined the Hampstead Pals in France to commemorate and celebrate his life.

Talking of hierarchy, or better still, 'Senior Officers' in the Metropolitan Police, I would like to express my thanks to John Grieve CBE QPM, my friend and companion to the battlefield on many tours including our Gallipoli adventure in 2015. A top man in his professional service in the Metropolitan Police, a lover of history and fine red wine, he has never failed to offer his help, support and battlefield artwork for this project.

Many thanks are also due to John Buoy, a retired schoolmaster and a fellow team mate in our youthful rugby-playing days, who contributed the chapter on fallen rugby footballers whom we commemorated in 2015. Likewise, Roger Smith and Mrs Jean Latham for their unfailing support. I would also mention my great friend Ian Alexander, himself a brilliant battlefield guide, who piped at Joe Symon's ashes-placing in France and who warmly employed me often - and paid me generously - as a battlefield guide for his excellent *War Research Society* for many years. Ian, a retired Detective Sergeant in the Birmingham City Police, sadly departed this life in 2018. I miss him.

It would also be appropriate to mention here by name the guides and historians (other than John Grieve) who have assisted the Pals by generously sharing their knowledge of the Great War soldiers and battlefields over the years and consequently journeyed with the Hampstead Pals, namely Willie Mohan, Kevin Cutts, Colin Butler MBE, Mary Ellen Freeman, Anthony Spagnoly, Steve Page, Mary Roche, Peter Barton and Clive Harris. A warm thank you is also due to our main advisor at The Commonwealth War Graves Commission, Nigel Stevens, who unstintingly joined our coach on many happy days in France and gave proper first-hand advice on the work of the Commission. I would also like to thank the Pals who have taken many of the photos published in this book, mainly Sue Brown, Bill Gemmell and Keith Collman. I must also thank Publishers, *AA Knopf*, for permission to quote from 'The Other Side and other Poems by Gilbert Frankau'. Plus, Edward Arnold (Publishers) Ltd for permission to quote 'Picardie' by Alys Fane Trotter. Routledge for permission to quote the powerful short poem from 'A Social History of English Rugby' by Tony Collins. Much inspiration was taken from 'Into Touch' *Rugby Internationals killed during the First World War* by Nigel McCrery (Pen & Sword 2014). The prime source being, 'Rugby Football Internationals Roll of Honour' by EHD Sewell (1919) Not forgetting an old friend, Mike Jackson, for his diligent research on individual soldiers. Last but certainly not least, to my wife, Linda, for her unfailing support and in reading and advising on the early drafts and contributions.

Jonathan Nicholls April 2022

Further acknowledgements.

This project would not have been possible without the contributions of the Hampstead Pals themselves - not all police officers - some of whom have made powerful and moving tributes to 'lost' family members. They are duly recorded in the index at the front of the book.

Through a period of 43 years, over 350 pilgrims have 'sailed' with the Hampstead Pals, some only once, but many come back year after year. You know who you are and we thank you for your undying support. There are many sunny memories.

Here are their names, not in any particular order, with sincere apologies to those I have left out through memory loss due to advancing years or mentioned twice, in which case blame *The Dalmore*.

Michael Curtis, Peter Dumville, John Steedman, Ian Menzies, Frank Yeates, Sam Klok, Nick Compton, Perry Spivey, Paul Hewetson, Maurice Link, Peter Gilhooley, Chris Wilkinson, Sheila Wilkinson, Ted Clarke, Barry Hamilton, Jim Hobbs, Douglas Mackenzie, Roger Evans, Steve Gilbert, Stan Uzzell, Colin Butler, Mary Freeman, Peter Barton, John Stevens, Cressida Dick, John Amos, Trevor Bettles, Willie Mohan, Dave Beck, Alan Oliver, Mandy Oliver, Anthony Spagnoly, Clive Harris, John Grieve, Gilli Grieve, Philip Grieve, Rorie Grieve, Bruce Colman, Gloria Ewan, Paul Nicolas, Anne Harvey, Jean Latham, Nick Batt, Brian Batt, Dominic Batt, Lewis Batt, Anita Owen, Barbara Middleton, Julia Bashford, Barbara Bashford, John Hickie, Terry Wilson, Lee Reboul, Bill Reboul, Bill Gemmel, Kevin Hall, Mark Nicholls, Cyril Nicholls, Dora Nicholls, Rory White, Michael How, Rick Jackson, Eugenie Brooks, Alwyn Jones, Meirion Hughes, Peter Copley, Anne Copley, John Nicholls, Roger Smith, Celia Smith, Ian Woledge, Jonathan Green, Ray Schofield-Almond, Paul Schofield-Almond, Charlie Tyler, Howard French, Andrew Dumville, Greg Nicholls, Anne Moody, Gilly Shorter, Alan Shorter, Sue Brown, Barry Brown, Judith Rushby, Caroline Carr, Jacqui Downing, Jackie Canvin, Stuart Chambers, Stuart Clarke, Les Guest, Edna Guest, Jamie Hardwick, Joe Brown, Jim Matthews, Derek Bloomfield, Alan Tolchard, Alex Rudelhoff, Brian Keys, Bob Hainey, Jim Hainey, Barney Doyle, Richard Graham, Elspeth Graham, Mary Wooderson, David Yeo, John McCauley, Dave Taylor, Dave Edwards, Lorraine Edwards, Steve Randall, Alison Johnstone, Bruce Dobson, Raymond Carr, Paul Carr, Susan Carr, Joe Symon, Greg Symon, Carol Chaffey, Mary Halsey, Nick Richardson, Chris Busby, George Busby, Cheryl Cummings, Chris

Armstrong, Kathleen Crowe, Graham Finnis, Geoff Butler, David Fisher, Sally Fisher, Janet Jones, Dave Hobart, Geoff Baker, Anne Flower, Ted Farrelly, Peter Crew, David Naden, Richard Varley, Richard Henninghem, Ralph Lewin, Keith Collman, Ronnie Macdonald, Jim Macdonald, John (Dick) West, Duncan West, Graeme West, Chris West, Christopher Quinton, Carol Quinton, John Buoy, Jan Buoy, Lesley Wyatt, Elaine Smyth, Grant Sidey, Carol Smale, Barry Phillips, Mick Freeman, John Mitchell, Trevor Colman, John Williams, Mick Maloney, John Jenkins, Mary Wallace, Robert Davy, Graham Yendall, Hilary Shotton, Roger Learney, Helen Learney, John Hine, Maureen Hine, Howard Pickard, John Cockram, Ian Lancaster, Jack Shults, Janine Wilson, John Broadbent, John Gleeson, John Bailey, Pete Worville, Karen Worville, Julia Richardson, Mick Adams, Keith Anker, Julia Anker, Mick Andrews, Kevin Cutts, Claire Cutts, Coren Smith, Phyllis Smith, Alf Smith, Gordon Atkinson, Keith Boswell, Martin Cator, Lyn Birbeck, Ralph Millington, Martin Clarke, Mary Flowerdew, Nigel Stevens, Fred Hine, Peter Butterworth, Mike Olley, Ralph Heaviside, Rachel Macleod, Roger Price, Sean Wall, Steve Ashman, Steve Page, Kate Page, Eric Page, Terry Russell, Tony Clatworthy, Michael Conroy, Mike Jackson, Anne Jackson, Val Walter, John Pearse, John Cave, Elizabeth Cave, Kevin Bryan, Kevin Dunkley, Marilyn Taylor, Nick Gould, Tony Stackhouse, Phil Rambert, Phil Pearce, Bob Andrews, Ray Waters, Alf Razzell, Wyn Razzell, Bill Hay, Charlie Taylor, Jack Cousins, Bill Partridge, David Jones, Russell Garland, Patsy Gaster, John Gaster, Coral Minnifie, Mike Stanley, Colin Rudd, Jane Rudd, Jane Hayward, Bernard Williams, Bill Thorpe, Anne Thorpe, John Goodman, Bob Thompson, Jean Thompson, John Mansell, Mike 'Tex' Marshall, Jim Clark, John Field, Chris Mark, Ian Tottman, Martin Power, Terry White, Brian Baker, Ray Dunleavy, Ken Smith, Sue Smith, John Yarnel, Jo Bond, Andrew Seed, Mary Roche, Beulah Coombes, David Isaacs, Ken Warren, Shirley Jeffrey, Jonny Moore, Victor Sloan, Simon Hill-Gibbins, Bob Jeeves, Harry Pickering, Martin Cutts, Neville Slack, Penny Slack, Judy Reemer, Patricia Bishop, Colin Weaver, Ruth Hawkridge, Chris Coakley, Pat Toohey, Lars Ruby, Richard Kerr, Becky Hale, Jim Terry, Kate Nelson, Paul Wiseman, Anne Wiseman, John Blackwell, Karen Bermingham, Katie Williams, Kathy Stone, Keiron Murphy, Mark Sheehan, Georgia Sheehan, Debbie Wyatt, Grant Sidey, Keith Simpson, Teddy Noyes, Gary Croaker, Beryl Razzell, Eric Challis, Jill Challis, Sid Fox, George Clarke, Jarvis Browning, Pamela Holliday, Phillip Kilpin, Valerie Walter, Ken Evans, Ian Wilmot, Gary Wilmot, Paul Cotton, Jill Cotton, Peter Jones, Ray Needham, Jim Razzell, Ivena Lea, Lee Garland, John Tagg, Dave Morgan, Les Cheeseman, Dick Stephens, Gilli Grieve, Jeremy Parker, Iris Oakey,

Simon Briggs, David Catton, Nick Lilburn, John Goodwin, Dave Proctor, Jessie Proctor, Charlie Russell, Jan de Jong, Ian Ronson, Steve Maude, Dave Goodman, Andrew Johnson, George Collins, Steve Blundell, Una Blundell, Bernard Roberts, Peter Smith, Joy Smith, Wilf Schofield, Mike Messenger, Mary Messenger, Stella Truscott.

To find out more about The Hampstead Pals tours to the Western Front 1914-18 battlefields, please visit www.hampsteadpals.com